# The BEGGING PLACE

"For I know the plans that I have for you," declares the Lord, "plans for welfare and not for calamity to give you a future and a hope. Then you will call upon Me and come and pray to Me, and I will listen to you. And you will seek Me and find Me when you search for Me with all your heart" (Jeremiah 29:11-3).

## ACKNOWLEDGMENTS

*To my sweet husband Jeff, who encouraged me every step of the way and worked so diligently for the book's success. You will always be my forever friend.*

*To my wonderful children, Jennifer and Jeffrey, who have surrounded me with unconditional love and glorious laughter.*

*To my dear sisters who have prayed for this book— what would I do without you in my life?*

*To my mother, Lea Fowler: This is especially for you, Mom. You will always be my best friend, my soul mate, and my best Bible teacher. What a privilege and honor it is to be called your daughter!*

LEA FOWLER, 1942

# The BEGGING PLACE

## A Book about Prayer for Christian Women

# Becky Blackmon

Publishing Designs, Inc.
Huntsville, Alabama

Publishing Designs, Inc.
P.O. Box 3241
Huntsville, Alabama 35810

Second Printing: January 2008
Third Printing: August 2009
Fourth Printing: January 2012
Fifth Printing: June 2014
Printed in the United States of America

---

Library of Congress Cataloging-In-Publication Data

Blackmon, Becky, 1948-
  The begging place / Becky Blackmon.
    p. cm.
  ISBN 0-929540-57-3 (alk. paper)
  1. Prayer—Christianity. 2. Prayer—Biblical teaching.  I. Title.
  BV210.3.B55 2007
  248.3'2—dc22
                    2006101203

---

## DEDICATION

To my Father in Heaven

# CONTENTS

# MEET THE FOWLERS

## HER LAP

I was raised on my mother's lap. It was simply "my spot." I was the third child in a very busy family, and the only time Mom and I had to bond was in church. Since we were there at least three times a week for several hours, that lap was my claim to Mom. Church was "our time," and no one dared to infringe on my territory.

That lap was specially made, you know. Surely, all children feel this way. Mother's lap has just the right natural folds and cushions. It is always "just right" for young'uns. You know what I mean. God certainly knew what He was doing when He created it. Mom's lap was my comfort, my peace, and all mine.

I grew up surrounded by love. My brother, sister, and I were constantly hugged, kissed, and encouraged. However, discipline was plentiful—we had a red-haired mama with a short fuse. And we were red-headed kids up to no good. Life at the Fowler home was exciting, I am sure, to our many friends and visitors.

Mom's magnetic personality drew people to her. She loved people, loved being around people. She had a fantastic sense of humor that not only made her laugh (even at herself) but caused others to laugh as well. Like Lucille Ball, she was just naturally funny. In fact, we often called her "Lucy."

Were we a typical American family? I don't think so, as I look back upon those years. Why not? Because God was the hub of our family, and His will was to be obeyed. The Bible was, and still is, precious to us. I have countless memories of Bible discussions and personal Bible studies at our kitchen table. My parents were true missionaries. They looked for people who needed the gospel; they used every possible opportunity to talk about the Lord; they went into mission fields to convert the lost. One of my later memories of my parents is hearing them read and discuss their daily Bible chapters.

As a teenager, I once expressed to my mother how wonderful it would be to live in Europe and travel constantly from country to country. She replied, "If you do that, how will you grow spiritually? How will you be able to help the church? You will not have a home congregation that needs you and your money to grow. You will not be able to take advantage of the classes and study times that are offered because you are too busy traveling." Did she know how to burst a bubble! But she was right.

## MOM

Lea Emma Reid was born in Delaware, Oklahoma, the eldest of three children. Mom's mother died in her early thirties, leaving the three children in the care of her husband. They were a humorous family, full of laughter and practical jokes, and constant singing. Grandfather played just about any instrument and had a repertoire of vaudeville songs. At age fourteen, he ran away from home and joined a circus band. Like George Burns, he would do a little tap dance and say, "Hey, kids, have I ever sung the song about a million-dollar baby?" At family reunions we children listened in awe to my grandfather's tales of his three children's shenanigans.

My mother was never spanked. Her father could not bring himself to physically punish any of his children. He would only say, "Did you learn your lesson?" (This was always puzzling to me since Mom would beat the fire out of her own children. When I reminded her that she was never spanked, she replied, "Well, I always knew I needed it!" That did not help much.)

## DAD

Russell William Fowler was born in Eakley, Oklahoma, into a hard-working farm family of nine children. The boys rose early and went to the field while the girls cooked, cleaned, and cared for the men when they came home. My grandmother, a little German woman, was a wonderful cook. She cooked homemade bread daily that deliciously melted in the mouth. She loved *National Geographic* magazines—had wallpapered an entire room in her home with its maps. She had many grandchildren, and she called all the granddaughters "Sister" or "Sissy." The family was no stranger to tragedy. Daddy's father died too early from a heart attack. My dad, only fourteen at the time, quietly shouldered the responsibility of maintaining the farm. On the heels of the tragedy of his Father's death came the Great Depression.

## RELIGIOUS BACKGROUNDS

Both my parents were raised in strong Baptist homes. My dad told many stories of riding in a wagon or a Model T to the church in town. Mom was a city girl in Tulsa and worshiped at the big Baptist church in the middle of town where the preacher wore a tuxedo every Sunday. Mom was born to do mission work. She reminisced about walking down the aisle with tears streaming down her face during an altar call for missionary hopefuls.

When my mother was nearing twenty, she visited a cousin in Borger, Texas. What a change of scenery! She left grass and lush trees and came to no grass and no trees. Borger was an oil boom town, and Mom often said it was a wild place in the '40s. Her cousin Della, a member of the church of Christ, invited Mom to go to church with her. Mom was delighted, secretly hoping there would be speaking in tongues and all kinds of gyrations.

Contrary to what she supposed, Mom found the church of Christ to be open, simple, honest, and interesting. There was no "show." The Bible was their only guide. Mom began the habit of underlining passages that conflicted with her belief, particularly passages in the New Testament. After listening and studying, she knew she had to make a change in her life. She did not know how her father would react, but she knew she had to become a member of the church that traced its roots back to the day of Pentecost. Mom paid quite a price for becoming a Christian; her father never forgave her.

## THE SPARKS FLY!

Soon after she became a Christian, my mother met my father. She was engaged to Noel, but on a double date Mom met his roommate, Russell. Their eyes met, and Mom said, "Hello, Russell." Dad said he knew immediately he was in love with her by the way she said his name. Mom said she knew her engagement to Noel was history. Here, in a booming and wild place in west Texas, God saw fit to bring two souls—two absolutely opposite people—together.

Mom and Dad dated six weeks and then married. Mom started studying the Bible with Dad, and soon he obeyed the same gospel the Ethiopian eunuch obeyed in Acts 8. We children teased them about getting married so quickly. "What was the rush?" we asked. Mom always said something like, "We were away from home, but I don't advise getting married so quickly."

## THE TORTOISE AND THE HARE

Mom and Dad had a great love for each other, full of passion. But they were also full of differences like the tortoise and the hare. Dad was the tortoise, slow moving and slow talking, methodically going about his day. Mom was the rabbit, bouncing here, bouncing there, and making life fun and exciting. It is hard for a turtle and a jackrabbit to understand each other, but after sixty-two years, their love was still mighty strong and passionate. They may not have been soul mates when they began, but they definitely were when their lives together came to an end.

My parents wanted lots of children, but God knew that three were all they could handle. My brother Tom was born in Phillips, Texas; Judy, in Tulsa during World War II; and I, in Andrews, Texas, after the war. Our home was Grand Central Station. Guests, visitors, and friends were always there. Mom was a wonderful hostess, extremely hospitable. Even when we were small children, she and Dad devoted Sunday nights to "fellowship" meetings for the teenagers of the church. We were promptly put to bed and went to sleep to the sound of laughter and the smell of the popcorn.

Dad, an accomplished welder, provided very well for us. Dad worked for Halliburton in Marlow, Oklahoma. He became a young elder in the church at Marlow. Our spiritual and social lives centered around the church: worship, vacation Bible schools, dinners on the grounds, lake parties, and the like. Life was great but things were about to change.

## THE MISSION BUG BITES

A new preacher and his wife moved to our congregation. Charles and Sue Chandler quickly became close family friends. They had done mission work in New England and planned on going back as soon as possible. They loved New England; they even cried when they saw a picture of the Northeast countryside. We thought that was funny, but later we changed our minds. Naturally, the Chandlers' experiences in evangelism drew our families closer until my parents finally decided to visit the Northeast.

I shall never forget the summer of '57. We packed our huge and long Pontiac station wagon and headed to New England for a two-week vacation. (That trip alone is worthy of a book.) I will never forget the beauty of New England. I had never seen the ocean and I had never seen mountains as beautiful as the White Mountains of New Hampshire. We traveled through town after town that did not have a church of Christ. My parents looked at each other in disbelief. There were only six congregations of the Lord's body in the New England states—Vermont, New Hampshire, Massachusetts, Connecticut, Maine, and Rhode Island. While on this vacation, my parents, passionate for the Lord's work, decided to move to the Northeast.

Mom, the rabbit, was ready to move immediately. Dad, the turtle, insisted on waiting until he could collect his retirement from Halliburton. During a family discussion, my brother Tom asked, "Dad, if we wait until you retire, what will happen to all those people who would have become Christians if we had moved sooner?" Tom's question turned the tide. Nothing more had to be said.

We went back to Marlow, sold everything we possibly could, and headed to New England in the same summer. We packed that oversized station wagon and pulled a U-Haul trailer filled with clothes, furniture, piano, freezer, dishes—all our treasures. Dad said we looked like a big turtle. Our adventure had begun and we would never be the same again.

## MY BROTHER TOM REMEMBERS

Dad had experienced an "epiphany" while we were at Springfield, Vermont, attending a singing. As we sang "Were You There When They Crucified My Lord," Dad just sat there beside Mom and wept silently. He knew that any expenses for his faith paled in comparison to Christ's investment in him.

He had already brought up the financial facts of the thing, and made a pretty good case for delaying our going until he had a nest egg called "retirement." However, we all recognized that the need was immediate, and waiting for retirement would mean that we kids would be gone, which might have been a desirable thing, from his perspective.

I asked, "How many might be saved in the years in between?" I was pretty doctrinaire, and things were more black and white for me. Obviously, I had no idea of the hardships that lay ahead. I did not have the burden of bills upon me. Dad did. He had no answer to my question. He wanted to answer, but he could not.

We made the move. I think we all knew that Dad had a huge load to carry in a land where we had no house and no job. His best friend came to bid him goodbye, and I could not bear to see Dad hug this friend. I looked down at the driveway, embarrassed. That is when I saw their tears wetting the concrete driveway beside the shadows of their embrace. That moment is still fresh in my mind. It made me understand a tiny bit the enormities of Dad's sacrifice and decision.

The Lord had opened a door, and a family that looked like a turtle drove through. We, too, soon learned to cry when we were away from New England and saw a picture of it. Mom often said, "When we moved to New England, we burned our bridges behind us. We got our feet stuck in the door and never looked back."

Once again, she was so right. We took to heart Jesus' words: "No one, after putting his hand to the plow and looking back, is fit for the kingdom of God" (Luke 9:62). We ate, breathed, slept, and lived evangelism. We children were taught always to be on our toes, looking for opportunities to help someone find his or her way home to God. We learned the value of the church for which Jesus died, and we saw the deep importance of the Word of God. In New England, we witnessed many baptisms and observed first-hand how lives can be changed for the Lord.

I am so thankful to God and to my sweet parents for choosing to move us to the Northeast. Growing up on the mission field was a great honor and a great blessing. We found this to be true: We grew up quickly. And, for the most part, we were spiritually deeper and more committed than other Christians our age. However, it was often difficult to find where we belonged.

I treasure the Bible my mother has passed on to me. She has written many wonderful notes all through it. Beside the passage in Luke 9:62 that we just read, she has penned, *You can't go forward looking back.*

And we never did.

My Mother was in a coma—unresponsive.
I called our good friend: "Fran, Mom is in a coma.
Please pray that God takes her now. She has suffered so
long. Beg for her to fly away." Fran replied with all the
sympathy a Christian can muster:
"I will go to the Begging Place."

# THE BEGGING PLACE

*Do you know the Begging Place? If you are a Christian, you should know it well. You have been there. Life has many lessons to teach us, but so does the Father. If you are a child of the King, an heir of salvation, God has many plans for you on earth. He knows what is ahead of you, and what decisions you will make. Above all, He knows the desires of your heart.*

The Begging Place *tells of my personal journey with God as His daughter. My story includes the amazing evidence of God's providence in my life, amidst much joy and much sadness. It reveals the special path I had to travel through the last days of my mother's life. Many memories still are painful. But God is the master of my life and the deliverer of my soul. This journey is not unusual because of death, for we all will lose our parents in this life, if Jesus does not come before then. The remarkable lesson is this: sadness and trials are not prohibited for the Christian; they produce a better Christian. And isn't that what God really wants us to be?*

*To please God, we must change and grow and suffer and mature. We learn our most valuable lessons when we are on our knees, when we turn to Him and let Him lead. When we truly become His sheep and trust Him as our Shepherd, we are the most blessed people in the world. Sheep have learned the power of prayer. Sheep have been to the Begging Place. Are you a sheep?*

## CHAPTER 1

# PRAYER CHANGES THINGS

*Elijah was a man with a nature like ours, and he prayed
earnestly that it might not rain; and it did not rain on
the earth for three years and six months. And he prayed
again, and the sky poured rain, and the earth produced
its fruit (James 5:17-18).*

As I was packing up my parents' home after their deaths, I stood gazing at Mom's kitchen window. As she did the dishes, she loved to look at the small objects that lined the windowsill. One was a little sign—a few words in a frame that held meaning for her: "Prayer changes things." Oh, how it does.

Perhaps you are wondering about prayer. What does prayer do? Maybe you are at the end of your rope. Is your life a mess? Do you see no hope for the future? Please take a moment and breathe deeply. Together, you and I will search the Scriptures for help. Praying is to the Christian as breathing is to the human. We cannot survive without talking to God. Prayer is the stuff from which strong Christians are made.

When did prayer start? Why did God give us the Begging Place? How many people today really pray? These are just a few questions all humans ask at one time or another.

I found these figures to be interesting. According to a study by the Barna Research Group, from 1991 to 2001, 82 percent of adults and 89 percent of teenagers pray in a normal week. Eighty-eight percent of the women and 75 percent of the men pray in a normal week (Mack Lyon, *In Search of the Lord's Way*, May 2005, 36).

God created man and woman, and He knew from the very beginning that we would need Him. He knows it is human nature to worry and fret because He knows our minds, and He knows our lives. From the very beginning, God has wanted men and women to seek Him. Prayer is our opportunity to meet God and lay our burdens upon Him. Prayer opens the door to building a relationship with the Master, to surrendering our burdens to His care, and to receiving the peace of mind only the Father can bestow. And let us not forget that through prayer we can praise our Father and thank Him for His many blessings. Mack Lyon put it this way:

> About the first thing that needs to be said about prayer is that it is an antidote, a corrective, or a cure for worry. It is a sincere form of the recognition of God and His very being, who is, who He is, His nature, and His personal presence in our day-to-day world. It's also an invitation to Him who is all-knowing, infinitely wise, and almighty to take charge of the things that trouble us or provoke us to worry (Mack Lyon, *In Search of the Lord's Way*, May 2005, 45).

## BACK TO THE BEGINNING OF TIME

God has always desired a relationship with mankind, and mankind has always desired a relationship with God. God enjoyed walking and talking with Adam and Eve. The Creator of the universe customarily met the created in the cool of the day. They had the honor and privilege of communicating directly with God.

After Adam and Eve sinned, God came looking for them: "And they heard the sound of the Lord God walking in the garden in the cool of the day, and the man and his wife hid themselves from the presence of the Lord God among the trees of the garden" (Genesis 3:8).

Because of their sin, Adam and Eve were hiding, fearful for the very first time in their lives. Their relationship with God had changed.

> *Prayer is our opportunity to meet God and lay our burdens upon Him.*

Sin always changes any relationship with God. Why? Because it separates us from Him. Sin creates a huge, gaping barrier. Only repentance and getting our lives right with God can make that barrier disappear. It was that way for the first family, and it is the same for you and me. In our home, this was always called "keeping the slate clean." As kids, my brother and sister and I had not only to keep the slate clean with our parents, but also with our Father in heaven. Life just did not go well for us until we had made all things right.

What is amazing is that our Father in heaven, the most awesome master of the universe, is even interested in having a relationship with mankind! But He is. In his work on God's nature, Frank Chesser wrote:

> Man's very existence and nature offer further insight into the nature of God. God is a social being. The reality of man is proof thereof. God is love (1 John 4:8). Love demands an object. God created man as the object of His love. God loves man, and God greatly desires for man to love Him. Man's very being testifies to the social and loving nature of God (Frank Chesser, *Portrait of God* [Publishing Designs, Inc.: Huntsville, AL, 2004], 15).

Even after Adam and Eve were banished from the Garden of Eden, God continued to talk to them and to the patriarchs, judges, and prophets who came after them. Read your Old Testament and find the many times that God personally talked to Abraham, Moses, Joshua, David, Samuel, and Jeremiah. God did not hide from His people. He could always be reached.

## GOD OF THE HEBREWS

How did Moses know where to go when he led God's people out of Egypt? God guided him by providing a cloud by day and a pillar of fire by night. When the cloud stopped moving, Moses stopped. And when it was dark, Moses and the people could easily see the pillar of fire.

> And the Lord was going before them in a pillar of cloud by day to lead them on the way, and in a pillar of fire by night to give them light, that they might travel by day and by night. He did not take away the pillar of cloud by day, nor the pillar of fire by night, from before the people (Exodus 13:21–22).

When God was instructing Moses about the many laws by which His people were to live, He continually reassured Moses that He was with His people and among them. God wanted them to feel secure. Here are two examples:

> ✠ (Concerning leprosy) "You shall send away both male and female; you shall send them outside the camp so that they will not defile their camp where I dwell in their midst" (Numbers 5:3).

✠ "And you shall not defile the land in which you live, in the midst of which I dwell; for I the Lord am dwelling in the midst of the sons of Israel" (Numbers 35:34).

God has always loved His people, even when they were unfaithful and disobedient. (That is amazing!) We know He provided manna and quail and water to the children of Israel, even when they wandered in the wilderness for forty years because of their unbelief. He still loved His people. Consider the following verses from Nehemiah 9 and notice God's unfailing love and deliverance:

> O may Thy glorious name be blessed and exalted above all blessing and praise! Thou alone art the Lord. Thou hast made the heavens, the heaven of heavens with all their host, the earth and all that is on it, the seas and all that is in them. Thou dost give life to all of them and the heavenly host bows down before Thee . . . Thou didst see the affliction of our fathers in Egypt, and didst hear their cry by the Red Sea. Then Thou didst perform signs and wonders against Pharaoh, against all his servants and all the people of his land; . . . and thou didst make a name for Thyself as it is this day. And Thou didst divide the sea before them, so they passed through the midst of the sea on dry ground; and their pursuers Thou didst hurl into the depths, like a stone into raging waters. And with a pillar of cloud Thou didst lead them by day, and with a pillar of fire by night to light for them the way in which they were to go. Then thou didst come down on Mount Sinai, and didst speak with them from heaven; Thou didst give to them just ordinances and true laws, good statutes and commandments. So Thou didst make known to them Thy holy sabbath, and didst lay down for them commandments, statutes, and law, through Thy servant Moses. Thou didst provide bread from heaven for them for their hunger, Thou didst bring forth water from a rock for them for their thirst, and Thou didst tell them to enter in order to possess the land which Thou didst swear to give them. But they, our fathers, acted arrogantly; they became stubborn and would not listen to Thy commandments. And they refused to listen, and did not remember Thy wondrous deeds which Thou hadst performed among them; so they became stubborn and appointed a leader to return to their slavery in Egypt. But Thou art a God of forgiveness,

> "Thou art a God of forgiveness . . . slow to anger, and abounding in loving-kindness . . . Thou didst not forsake them.

gracious and compassionate, slow to anger, and abounding in lovingkindness; and Thou didst not forsake them. Even when they
made for themselves a calf of molten metal and said, "This is your
god who brought you up from Egypt," and committed great blas-
phemies, Thou, in Thy great compassion, didst not forsake them
in the wilderness; the pillar of cloud did not leave them by day, to
guide them on their way, nor the pillar of fire by night, to light for
them the way in which they were to go. And Thou didst give Thy
good Spirit to instruct them, Thy manna Thou didst not withhold
from their mouth, and Thou didst give them water for their thirst.
Indeed, forty years Thou didst provide for them in the wilderness
and they were not in want, their clothes did not wear out, nor did
their feet swell . . . However, Thou didst bear with them for many
years, and admonished them by Thy Spirit through Thy prophets,
yet they would not give ear. Therefore Thou didst give them into the
hand of the peoples of the lands. Nevertheless, in Thy great compassion Thou didst not make an end of them or forsake them, for
Thou art a gracious and compassionate God (Nehemiah 9:5–31).

God spoke directly to the fathers and prophets of the Patriarchal
Age and the Mosaic Age. Throughout the Old Testament we see over
and over again how much God loved Israel, His chosen nation. However, her continual spiritual adultery and idolatrous worship caused
her eventual downfall and captivity.

God, after He spoke long ago to the fathers in the prophets in many
portions and in many ways, in these last days has spoken to us
in His Son, whom He appointed heir of all things, through whom
also He made the world (Hebrews 1:1–2).

Are we living in the Patriarchal or Mosaic Age now? No. God
promised in Genesis 3:15 that the seed of woman would bruise
Satan's head. In other words, the Messiah would come to earth and
save mankind. This was God's scheme of redemption. Jesus changed
everything when He came to earth, was crucified, buried, and rose
on the third day. On the day of Pentecost, the Christian Age was ushered in, and the church of Christ was established (Acts 2:47; Romans
16:16).

Even during the first days of the church, God still wanted the
Jews to be a part of that kingdom for which Jesus died. It was the
Jews who heard the first gospel sermon preached on Pentecost by
the apostle Peter. Over and over we read in the Bible how Paul would
enter a city and immediately go to the local synagogue where he

convinced Jews that Jesus was the Messiah. Here is his message to the Romans: "For I am not ashamed of the gospel, for it is the power of God for salvation to everyone who believes, to the Jew first and also to the Greek" (Romans 1:16).

Paul explained to the Greeks gathered on Mars' Hill:

> He made from one, every nation of mankind to live on all the face of the earth, having determined their appointed times, and the boundaries of their habitation, that they should seek God, if perhaps they might grope for Him and find Him, though He is not far from each one of us (Acts 17:27).

God made all the nations of the world by means of one man, Adam. Is not Adam called the father of mankind today? This Scripture says God had already determined what nations would appear, where they would live, and how long they would exist. God has also determined that nations—humans—should seek God. Note the conditional verb *should*. The translation is "should," not "shall"! Nations and people should seek God, but we know realistically that not all seek Him.

> *"They should seek God . . . grope for Him and find Him, though He is not far from each one of us.*

Now let's think about that last phrase of verse 27: "He is not far from each one of us." Who is not far from us? God. The Father, the Creator, is always near. He has not abandoned His creation; He promised that He will always be close to us.

One of the most wonderful "comfort" passages in the whole Bible is: "Let your character be free from the love of money, being content with what you have; for He Himself has said, "I will never desert you, nor will I ever forsake you" (Hebrews 13:5).

## GETTING TO KNOW THE FATHER

Does it surprise you that the Father wants a relationship with you? It most certainly surprises me! However, I am absolutely positive that I want a very close and personal relationship with Him. I believe that most Christians do. God the Son stands at the door of our hearts and knocks, desiring a home with us. He will never force His way in. The choice is ours. We either let Him in or we leave Him out in the cold:

Behold, I stand at the door and knock; if anyone hears My voice and opens the door, I will come in to him, and will dine with him, and he with Me. He who overcomes, I will grant to him to sit down with Me on My throne, as I also overcame and sat down with My Father on His throne (Revelation 3:20–21).

When I was a child, I loved to look at the beautiful pictures in Bibles: The Good Shepherd with a lamb in His arms, Jesus on the cross, Pharaoh's daughter finding baby Moses in the bulrushes, Moses on Mt. Sinai, and Jesus praying in Gethsemane, just to name a few. But the picture of Jesus standing and knocking at a door that only opened from the inside was the most intriguing to me.

Come to Me, all who are weary and heavy-laden, and I will give you rest. Take My yoke upon you and learn from Me, for I am gentle and humble in heart, and you shall find rest for your souls. For My yoke is easy, and My load is light (Matthew 11:28–30).

Jesus' call two thousand years ago still has an impact on hearts searching for peace and rest. In fact, I believe His words are even more powerful and meaningful to us now living in this stressful, demanding, fast-paced twenty-first century! Christ's pleas for mankind to surrender to Him are still as pertinent and touching today as when He walked upon earth.

I am a Christian, and my desire is to please God every way I possibly can. I have made my decision—I chose Him a long time ago. He is my Father; I am His daughter, and I want to know Him better. How do I achieve this? Well, there are two ways to know the Father better and to walk more closely with Him: pray and study His Word. This is where our relationship with Him begins.

## WHAT IS THE BEGGING PLACE?

The Begging Place is a place of prayer. However, prayers offered at the Begging Place are not typical supplications requesting quick, simple answers. It is one thing to pray, but it is an entirely different thing to beg, plead, implore. At the Begging Place hearts are poured out to God, often with many tears. It is a place of the deepest entreaty we can possibly offer up to Him. At the Begging Place our prayers are pleas of the deepest nature, as our lives are upset with conflict, problems, sin, and Satan's attacks. We have a reason to be there.

Frequently, we go to the Begging Place in behalf of someone we love. Parents will find themselves at God's door, begging for their children's lives or answers to their children's problems. Brothers and sisters in a church will pour out their hearts to God in behalf of another brother or sister with a serious illness or a grievous crisis. Many times we beg God to touch the hearts of unfaithful Christians. And we often go to the Begging Place to ask for forgiveness of sin. How many Christians have gone to the Begging Place because of broken hearts, broken dreams, and broken marriages?

> "He only is my rock and my salvation, my stronghold; I shall not be shaken.

Listen to this sweet song of David:

> My soul, wait in silence for God only, for my hope is from Him. He only is my rock and my salvation, my stronghold; I shall not be shaken. On God my salvation and my glory rest; the rock of my strength, my refuge is in God. Trust in Him at all times, O people; pour out your heart before Him; God is a refuge for us (Psalm 62:5–8).

David had an unusual relationship with God. He certainly knew how to pour out his heart before Him. Think of David, alone many a night on a hilltop, guarding his father's sheep. Think of David, the anointed, whom Saul hated and tried to kill. Think of David, the shepherd king, begging God for guidance as he ruled Israel. And think of David, as the father of problem children and the husband of many wives. Those factors in themselves demanded lots of prayers, wouldn't you say?

## PRAYERS OF FAITH

Paul was inspired to make a request of the church at Thessalonica: "Brethren, pray for us" (1 Thessalonians 5:25). Read all of chapter 5, and you will sense the urgency of Paul's request. Specifically he said, "Pray without ceasing" (1 Thessalonians 5:17). We can gather from these two passages that Paul was most certainly coveting the prayers of the brethren in troubled times of the church and teaching the necessity of prayer in a Christian's life.

Listen to James, the brother of Jesus:

Is anyone among you suffering? Let him pray. Is anyone cheerful?
Let him sing praises. Is anyone among you sick? Let him call for the
elders of the church, and let them pray over him, anointing him
with oil in the name of the Lord; and the prayer offered in faith
will restore the one who is sick, and the Lord will raise him up,
and if he has committed sins, they will be forgiven him. Therefore,
confess your sins to one another and pray for one another, so that
you may be healed. The effective prayer of a righteous man can
accomplish much. Elijah was a man with a nature like ours, and
he prayed earnestly that it might not rain; and it did not rain on
the earth for three years and six months. And he prayed again,
and the sky poured rain, and the earth produced its fruit (James
5:13–18).

What is the meaning of "the prayer offered in faith"? How does
one do that? By praying, knowing that God can fix the problem. We
pray with faith, knowing that God is hearing our prayer and answering it also. So we are living the Scripture: "For we walk by faith, not
by sight" (2 Corinthians 5:7).

Our preacher once told a story about Parker, his young grandson. Parker's grandmother was sick, and Parker told his grandfather,
"Grandmother is going to get better." His grandfather asked, "How
do you know this, Parker?" The reply was quick and sure: "Because I
prayed for her." Now folks, that prayer was offered in faith!

## Encouragement of the Scriptures

Let's examine James' mention of Elijah. The Scriptures say that
Elijah had a nature like ours—which means he was just like us. Eli-
jah also prayed earnestly. What does that mean? Sincerely. Devoutly.
Soberly. Could it be that Elijah went to the Begging Place, too? While
we do not know the details, we do know this: God heard and granted
Elijah's request! Was Elijah's prayer a simple request? I do not believe
so because requesting no rain has a huge effect on the earth, and the
Scripture says it did not rain for three and a half years.

The Bible tells us of quite a few people who went to the Begging
Place with a desperate request of the Lord. We are going to look at six
exemplary accounts—Hannah, Hezekiah, Esther, David, Jesus, and
Cornelius. These events from the Book are given to demonstrate that

God is ever present in our lives, working things out for our good. Two of my favorite Scriptures are:

- "For whatever was written in earlier times was written for our instruction, that through perseverance and the encouragement of the Scriptures, we might have hope" (Romans 15:4).
- "And we know that God causes all things to work together for good to those who love God, to those who are called according to His purpose" (Romans 8:28).

Our Father has not left us in the dark. He has given us a wealth of information to help us persevere and be encouraged. But most of all, these Scriptures will give us hope. What a wonderful word—*hope*. What did Paul mean by "Scriptures"? The Old Testament. The early Christians did not have a completed New Testament. Now we have God's entire revelation—the Old Testament and the New Testament—to give us even more hope.

## The Bad Times

What defines us as children of God is not how we handle the good times, but how we handle the bad times. Anyone can adjust to a life full of good days and money in the bank. That's a day in the park! It is when we are tested or tempted that we show our true colors—our real selves. Where do we turn when we are upset, when our lives are full of troubles, and when Satan hurls catastrophes at us? Do we immediately seek our Father in prayer and run to the Bible for help, solace, and teaching? In troubled times we learn to bow before our awesome Father and beg for deliverance. We turn to our source of strength—God.

> It is when we are tested or tempted that we show our true colors—our real selves.

I have a dear sister in Georgia named Belle. Yes, she is a true Southern belle. She is also a mighty servant of the Lord—a doer. She is one of those types of gals who just "appear" when you need someone the most. She is very intuitive and sensitive and loving. She is unafraid to show her emotions or to say what she truly thinks—always in love, of course.

Belle has just been diagnosed with a malignant brain tumor, and my heart is heavy for her and for me. I talked to her today and once again, her positive outlook on life is reigning supreme. She told me, "I am ready for whatever the Lord has planned for me. He has another life ready for me, and His will is best."

When I asked her about her prayer life, she replied, "I have learned how to pray. I thought I knew how, but I had never been sick before. Now I know how to pray."

Belle has been to the Begging Place. And those of us who know her and love her have been to the Begging Place on her behalf.

## IT'S ALL ABOUT HIM

Whatever happens to us, no matter how bad it is, God will work it out for our good. The world often misquotes that great Romans passage: "Everything will work together for good." That is not what the Bible says. God issues two conditions. God will cause all things to work out for those who love Him and those who are the called according to His purpose—God's purpose, not man's. In order for God to bless us and work out our problems, we must love Him and do His will. It is all about Him and not us, my friend! God is the only one who can take something absolutely horrible and turn it into something positive and beneficial for His children. He is near; all we must do is draw near.

## DRAW NIGH UNTO GOD

In the quietness 'mid the stillness
We commune as friend with friend.
He is near us, He will hear us
As long as time extends.

When the busy rush of Life around us
Captures all our needs and cares.
We speak those words within our hearts,
Because we know He is there.

When the early sun awakens
Over the distant hill,
The sun breaks forth with many colors
Everything is so quiet and so still.

In these peaceful moments of our Lives
We pause and talk to Him in prayer.
We know that God is listening
Because He is always there.

—Mary Margerum

When we meet God at the Begging Place, we pray in faith, knowing He hears and answers our cries. We are never alone there. We bare our soul to our Father, and we are unashamed to beg at His feet. There is hope at the Begging Place because "with God all things are possible" (Matthew 19:26). My dad used to say, "With God the impossible is possible!"

There is one very important fact to consider here: the act of praying is as serious as it can possibly be. When we pray, we approach the throne of God; we are in His presence. And like Moses, we are on holy ground. "Let us therefore draw near with confidence to the throne of grace, that we may receive mercy and find grace to help in time of need" (Hebrews 4:16).

## THOUGHTS TO PONDER

1. Why do we pray?

2. Name five ways God cared for the Israelites in the wilderness.

3. Why don't we live under the Old Law today?

4. What does it mean to pour out one's soul to God?

## SONG FOR TODAY

### WHAT A FRIEND WE HAVE IN JESUS

What a Friend we have in Jesus,
All our sins and griefs to bear!
What a privilege to carry
Ev'rything to God in prayer!
O what peace we often forfeit,
O what needless pain we bear,
All because we do not carry
Ev'rything to God in prayer.

Have we trials and temptations?
Is there trouble anywhere?
We should never be discouraged;
Take it to the Lord in prayer.
Can we find a friend so faithful,
Who will all our sorrows share?
Jesus knows our ev'ry weakness;
Take it to the Lord in prayer.

Are we weak and heavy laden,
Cumbered with a load of care?
Precious Savior, still our refuge—
Take it to the Lord in prayer.
Do thy friends despise, forsake thee?
Take it to the Lord in prayer;
In His arms He'll take and shield thee;
Thou wilt find a solace there.

## PRAYER FOR TODAY

*Dear Father, we praise Your Holy Name and give You all the glory. You spoke this world into existence and created us so tenderly. We are Your children and the sheep of Your pasture.*

*We thank You for Your magnificent love in sending Your Son Jesus to this earth to die for our sins. And though there was no room in the inn for Him, please help me always to have room for Him in my heart. Oh, never let me keep Him standing out in the cold, dear Father, but may I continually set His cross and His empty tomb before my eyes as constant reminders of Your incredible love.*

*Help me always to be sensitive to others and their needs. And help me to tell all that I meet about Jesus and His love for them. Thank You for this day, and help me to live for You tomorrow. Please forgive me of my sins, and help me to be more aware of them. In Jesus' name. Amen.*

# BECKY'S MEMORIES

## EARLY BEGGING PLACES

When I was a young girl, Mom and Dad went on one of their occasional hunting trips to Colorado. We three children were left with Mom and Dad's best friends, the Montgomerys. Nita and George lived in Marlow, Oklahoma, where we lived and worshiped together. Their three children, Leroy, Jerry, and Linda, were close to our ages; their home was our home. Our mothers were "Lucy and Ethel." There was always an abundance of laughter anywhere they were.

All of a sudden, I had a horrible attack of tonsillitis—a high fever and a painful sore throat. Nita was a wonderful nurse. She swabbed my throat and took measures to lower my temperature. That night, as I slept on a hide-a-bed in my best friend Linda's bedroom, I awoke with the awareness of someone's kneeling beside my bed. It was Nita, her head bowed and her hands folded. I could not hear what she was saying, but I knew she was in a deep prayer to God. I lay there, watching her form as she prayed in the dark. She did not know I was awake and observing her. She was obviously deeply concerned about my health. After about ten minutes, she rose from her knees and left the room.

How could I ever forget that pivotal moment! It was then that I realized Nita loved me. She cared enough to pray for me. We never spoke about it. But the impression Nita made on my life that night was very significant. It was hard for me to imagine someone other than my parents praying for me. "Why would anyone do that?" I wondered. And then I realized she loved me as much as my own mother. She was concerned about me, and went to the Father on my behalf.

I was better the next day and very grateful for Nita's vigilant care and doctoring skills. The lesson I learned that night will forever be etched in my mind. When people love each other, they pray for each other. And when a child is sick, mothers and substitute mothers go to the Begging Place.

When I grew up and became a mother of two sweet children, this precious memory came flooding over me as I knelt by their beds. It became a habit of mine to kneel by my children's beds and pray for them in sickness and in health. In troubled times, too.

When my children left for college, the empty nest was difficult for me. I went into their rooms, knelt beside their beds, and prayed for them. Naturally I was praying for various things: for their safe care, for them to use wisdom in all things, and for their futures. There were also serious times of going to the Begging Place when they were sick or involved in unhealthy relationships. They were too far away from home for me to rescue. There was nothing I could do—except pray.

When you have children, you will pray—a lot. You will learn to "let go and let God." What else can you do? At times you will feel as if you have gone to hell and back because of your own children. In those times of devastating worry, you will discover a marvelous thing. Our God—the Omnipresent, the Omniscient, and the Omnipotent—is alive and well and delivering your children, just like He delivered you when you were their age. You will sink to your knees in gratitude to Him as you realize what might otherwise have happened to your children. And you will thank Him for His marvelous grace and mercy once again.

I personally learned what "trust in the Lord" really means. For years I had quoted Proverbs 3:5 incorrectly. I always told my sisters, "Trust in the Lord, and do not lean on your own understanding." But that is not what that Scripture says. It says: "Trust in the Lord *with all your heart*, and do not lean on your own understanding."

You see, any of us can say "I trust in the Lord" and then go about our business and continue to worry and fret. Look at it again. The proverb says to "trust in the Lord with *all* your heart." Ah, that is different, isn't it? What does it mean? It means one trusts completely, wholly in the Lord and does not doubt a thing—Becky's definition, of course. It means "I surrender all to God."

There are several instances in the Scripture that God speaks about our children and their children. These are passages of comfort to those of us who have children and naturally worry about their destiny. Let us meditate on one of them:

As for man, his days are like grass; as a flower of the field, so he flourishes. When the wind has passed over it, it is no more; and its place acknowledges it no longer. But the lovingkindness of the Lord is from everlasting to everlasting on those who fear Him, and His righteousness to children's children, to those who keep His covenant, and who remember His precepts to do them (Psalm 103:15–18).

Girls, the years are flying by and our lives are but vapors (James 4:14). We are like the flower that flourishes in the grass, here one day and gone the next. We are rocking our babies one moment and then rocking our grandbabies the next. Our short time on this planet must be spent wisely. And the wisest thing we mothers can do is to teach our children about the marvelous love of the Lord and His plans for them (Jeremiah 29:11–13). So as we are rocking our babies, let's do some wise talking and some sweet singing.

## CHAPTER 2

# THE GIFT OF PRAYER

*The eyes of the Lord are toward the righteous,*
*and His ears are open to their cry.*
*The face of the Lord is against evildoers, to cut off the*
*memory of them from the earth. The righteous cry and*
*the Lord hears, and delivers them*
*out of all their troubles. The Lord is near to the*
*brokenhearted, and saves those who are crushed in spirit*
*(Psalm 34:15-18).*

Talking to God brings great blessings. There is comfort and there is peace for the Christian who seeks the Father and His will. There is also confidence in knowing that there will be an answer to that prayer. Let us not forget His promise: "Draw near to God and He will draw near to you" (James 4:8).

In His famous *Sermon on the Mount*, Jesus gave us the model prayer. Wedged between His thoughts is a Scripture that we must not miss:

> And when you are praying, do not use meaningless repetition, as the Gentiles do, for they suppose that they will be heard for their many words. Therefore, do not be like them; for your Father knows what you need, before you ask Him (Matthew 6:7–8).

Did you catch that: "before you ask Him"? When does God know what I am getting ready to pray for and ask for? Before I even utter the request or prayer. He knows me, and He knows my thoughts, and He knows my heart.

Consider a similar Old Testament passage: "Even before there is a word on my tongue, behold, O Lord, Thou dost know it all (Psalm 139:4). Some might say, "Then why bother to pray if He already knows what I am going to say?" Because God wants us to talk to Him, seek Him, and have a relationship with Him. Evidently God wants us to ask! Remember, Jesus says in Matthew 7:7–8: "Ask, and it shall be given to you; seek, and you shall find; knock, and it shall be opened to you. For everyone who asks receives, and he who seeks finds, and to him who knocks it shall be opened."

God has two blessings for us when we seek Him in prayer:

If God's mercies came to us unasked, they would not be half as useful as they now are, when they have to be sought for. Now we get a double blessing, a blessing in the obtaining and a blessing in the seeking. The very act of prayer is a blessing (Charles Spurgeon, *The Power of Prayer* [Whitaker House: New Kensington, PA, 1996], 72).

How true! Prayer is a gift from our heavenly Father to carnal children, to us who have so much to learn and so much to change.

## TALK TO ME

We want our children to talk to us, even if we already know their needs. When their hearts are broken, ours are broken. We want to fix every problem we possibly can, but we want our children to be appreciative.

My mother and I had a wonderful and close relationship. On many occasions she would say, "Becky, I love you so much that I would love to give you the moon if I could. But it wouldn't be good for you to have the moon." Parents understand that. We would love to give our children everything their little hearts desire, but that would be too much for them to handle. It is too much for us to handle! We must be wise just as our Father is wise.

We are called "children of God" and not "teenagers of God" or "adults of God."

Talking to our children—no matter how old they are—brings us closer to them, and them to us. When we talk, we grow together. We are bonding, and our relationship deepens. Even when we know our children's needs and desires, we still let them ask because we want to be asked and because it is good for them to ask.

God gives us children so we can understand the parent-child relationship and how much He, our heavenly Father, loves us. I love my children with every fiber of my being. There is nothing I would not do for them. God must have the same feeling for His children, only more. He is greater than we.

## GOD'S LITTLE GIRLS

To be called a child of God is absolutely the most wonderful blessing we can receive! The apostle John was inspired to write: "See how great a love the Father has bestowed upon us, that we should be called children of God; and such we are" (1 John 3:1).

Notice that we are called "children of God" and not "teenagers of God" or "adults of God." Let's look into this a little further. How do we interact with children? We are more tolerant, more understanding, and more patient. When we see children do foolish things, we say, "Oh, well, they will grow out of this." This is the way our Father is with us. He is tolerant, understanding, patient, and merciful. He sees the silly things we indulge in and says, "I know you will grow up and put this away, too."

As I was putting the finishing touches on this book, the publisher and I were discussing the cover design. I loved the scene of the girl, the hat, and the ocean. I just was not happy with the person in the picture being a little girl. I wanted a silhouette of a woman. As my daughter was looking at the sample cover, I reiterated that I really wanted a woman pictured and not a little girl. Jennifer said, "Oh, Mom, we *are* God's little girls." Good point. End of discussion.

### FATHER TAKE MY HAND

Father, take my hand.
I'm scared and on my own.
In my heart I'm just
A little girl and all alone.

Give your all to Me, My child, and don't look back.
We'll make the journey together,
And nothing shall you lack.
Put your trust in Me and seek Me through prayer;
I am your Father—I will always be there.

—Lea Fowler and Becky Blackmon

The Father sees us as His and no one else's. He knows every little detail about us—the good and the bad—and He still loves us. God wants us to seek His face, to go to Him in prayer. David said: "Glory in His holy name; let the heart of those who seek the Lord be glad. Seek the Lord and His strength; seek His face continually" (Psalm 105:3–4).

## ETERNITY IN OUR HEARTS

Several years ago I found an interesting passage in Ecclesiastes. What a marvelous book! I urge women everywhere I go: "Stop and study this book, verse by verse. It will change your life!"

Wise King Solomon set out on a quest to find happiness in his life. He built huge palaces, designed vineyards and gardens, bought slaves and livestock, increased his wealth, and of course, had a large harem—seven hundred wives and three hundred concubines to be exact. Anything his eyes desired, he acquired (Ecclesiastes 2:10). He pursued life to its fullest, and with each quest he realized everything in life is vanity—fleeting, empty, like a vapor. And Solomon realized that no man, no matter how wise, could understand the mind of God.

If we were to pursue the same things Solomon once did, what would we discover? Vanity. Meaninglessness. Futility. Everything is empty if God is not there. But He has given us a special treasure:

> He has made everything appropriate in its time. He has also set eternity in their heart, yet so that man will not find out the work which God has done from the beginning even to the end (Ecclesiastes 3:11).

We can never know what God is going to do next or what His plans are. However, what about this "eternity in their heart"? Let's think about it for a moment. God has placed eternity in our hearts. Can you relate to these experiences? You find the dining room furniture of your dreams and you put it on layaway? Then on the day that furniture is delivered, you step back and think, "Well, I guess I like it. Maybe I need new drapes."

Or you fall in love with an outfit that looks great on you, and again you gradually pay it off. Then you bring it home, try it on, and say to yourself, "Is this the right jacket? I don't remember its looking like this." There is an emptiness inside you because you thought having that dress or that dining room set was going to bring you joy. You are not as happy as you thought you would be.

Has this ever happened to you? It is normal. The reason the outfit or the furniture did not bring you happiness is because things are just that: things. Things do not bring you happiness because God has placed eternity in your heart. The spiritual void in our hearts cannot be satisfied with things.

Try as we will, we can never make the shallow things of this earth fill that void in our hearts. We will never be happy with material things because God has created mankind to want Him. When we put God in our hearts and minds, that's substance! The void starts to fill up and we feel better. We can grow on that. When we seek Him through prayer and through His Word, we find true happiness, peace, and satisfaction— guaranteed. Then we realize: True joy is finding God!

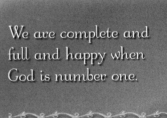

We are complete and full and happy when God is number one.

Solomon's statement in Ecclesiastes 12:13 shows this realization:

✠ "The conclusion, when all has been heard is: fear God and keep His commandments, because this applies to every person."

✠ "Fear God and keep His commandments, for this is man's all" (NKJV).

✠ "Fear God and keep his commandments, for this is the whole duty of man" (KJV).

In the King James Version the word *duty* has been added. The Hebrew text reads: "Fear God and keep His commandments, for this is the whole of man [or woman]." Our whole reason for living is to fear our God with reverential fear and to keep—obey faithfully—His laws. This is all of us. Fearing God and keeping His commandments are the whole of you and me. We are complete and full and happy when God is number one.

## COMMUNICATION

Ask any family therapist what all successful relationships must have, and he or she will reply, "Communication." People must talk to each other if they desire a loving marriage and family, a good friendship, or a compatible job relationship. Someone has to start talking.

Little girls start talking earlier than little boys do. And throughout life, females are more verbal than males. I have always wondered why God created men and women to be so different. (That is one of the first things I want to ask God when I get to heaven!) It is very difficult for us women to understand how men can be so totally opposite from us. Some say men are from Mars and women are from Venus. But it is as one homespun philosopher said: "Men are from earth and women are from earth. Deal with it!" Sometimes it seems like major surgery to get our husbands to talk to us. Research has shown that men use about one-fourth as many words daily as women use. And when men have used their portion, that's it. But we women just keep on talking—kind of like that Energizer bunny.

"Men are from earth and women are from earth. Deal with it!"

However, there is no excuse for either men or women not to talk to God. Our Father in heaven wants us to communicate with Him. If we desire a good and close relationship with Him, we must pray—and often. Too many times the following poem describes our prayer life.

### SWEET MINUTE OF PRAYER

Sweet minute of prayer! Sweet minute of prayer!
That's just about all I can spare.
I have regrets and lots of sin,
So I'll see if I can squeeze them in.
In seasons of distress and grief,
My greatest prayer is quick relief.
But things are swell, I've no despair,
I'll just spend half a minute in prayer.

—from the *Anglican Digest*

## PRAY ANYWAY

Matthew Henry, an eighteenth century Bible scholar, had this to say about prayer:

> Let no one insist that he cannot pray, for if you were ready to perish with hunger, you could beg and pray for food. Likewise, if you see yourself ruined because of sin, can you not beg and pray for mercy and grace? Are you a Christian? If so, never out of shame say, "I cannot pray," for that is as absurd as a soldier saying he does not know how to handle a sword, or a carpenter a saw. Why are you called into the fellowship of Christ, except that by Him you may have fellowship with God? Even if you cannot pray as well as others, pray as well as you can, and God will accept your prayers.
>
> Let no one plead that he does not have time in the morning for prayer. I dare say that you can find time for other things that are less needful; it would be better to take time from sleep than to lack time for prayer. How can you spend time better and more to your satisfaction and advantage? All the business of the day will prosper the better if you begin it in prayer with God.
>
> Let none plead that he does not have a convenient place to privately pray. Isaac retired into the field to pray. The psalmist could be alone with God in the corner of a housetop. If you cannot pray with as much secrecy as you would like, pray anyway. It is doing it with ostentation that is wrong, not doing it under observation when it cannot be avoided (Matthew Henry, *Experiencing God's Presence* [Whitaker House: New Kensington, PA, 1997], 52–53).

Remember that old saying: "There is no such a thing as an atheist in a foxhole!" Even an unbeliever, when his life is threatened, will usually call on God. Yes, he wants to live so much that he will even pray to the God he has often denied.

## BROTHER MARSHALL KEEBLE: "HAVE YOUR PHONE CONNECTED"

When I was sixteen, brother Marshall Keeble, a black preacher, came from Nashville, Tennessee, to Concord, New Hampshire, to hold a meeting. I had heard of him all of my life. My parents had heard him preach in Texas and Oklahoma many times. When I met him, he was in his eighties. My mother said he was her most honored guest. (That statement was extra complimentary because our home was Grand Central Station; Mom knew about having company.) Brother Keeble preached a week's meeting for our congregation and I had never heard such preaching. He changed my life. Those of you who had the honor and privilege of hearing brother Keeble understand. He spoke God's Word in such a way that you loved him. You even forgot about the clock on the wall. He was funny and witty one moment and then a spiritual powerhouse the next. My dad used to say, "You better watch it when brother Keeble makes you laugh, because his next sentence will step on your heart."

I will never forget one of brother Keeble's vivid prayer illustrations: "You know, praying to God is like having your phone connected to God. Praying is our hotline. My question is, do you have your phone connected?"

Praying should not be hard for women. We know how to communicate. We talk on the phone a lot; we "do lunch" together and talk. We don't have to be subjected to Chinese water torture to force us to talk. We will tell you what is wrong with our lives in a heartbeat. We know how to express ourselves, and we definitely know how to communicate our needs and desires. Just ask us. But the reality is that many women have problems talking to the Father.

## PRAYER TIES THAT BIND

Praying with my Christian sisters is indeed a wonderful experience. Many times I have sat with a circle of women, all of us weeping and pouring out our hearts to God. Those times are precious—never to be forgotten. And I have seen these prayers answered. Praying together binds you together. Charles Hodge once said, "The best gift you can give is to pray for someone."

The brother of our Lord wrote a powerful message: "Therefore, confess your sins to one another, and pray for one another, so that you may be healed. The effective prayer of a righteous man [or woman] can accomplish much" (James 5:16). The New King James Version says: "Confess your trespasses to one another, and pray for one another, that you may be healed. The effective, fervent prayer of a righteous man avails much."

> He who prays must be a righteous man. The prayer itself must be a fervent, in-wrought, well-wrought prayer. Such prayer avails much. It is of great advantage to ourselves, it may be very beneficial to our friends, and we are assured of its being acceptable to God . . . In prayer we must not look to the merit of man, but to the grace of God (Matthew Henry, *Matthew Henry Commentary on*

*the Whole Bible* [Zondervan Publishing House: Grand Rapids, MI, 1961], 1938).

## THE CRY OF THE RIGHTEOUS

How do you think God feels about prayer? Does it mean anything at all to Him? Of course it does. What does God desire to hear—the prayer of the sinful or the prayer of the righteous? Solomon tells us: "The sacrifice of the wicked is an abomination to the Lord, but the prayer of the upright is His delight" (Proverbs 15:8). This passage prompts us to examine our lives to see if we are upright, because we want God to listen to our pleas and supplications. We desire God's attention.

> "The righteous cry and the Lord hears, and delivers them out of all their troubles."

Listen to me on this. If you have a problem, who do you really want pleading your case? Your Christian family, of course. You want those who are attuned to God and are spiritually mature to ask of God in your behalf, don't you? It is absurd to think that Christians would ask the world or unfaithful Christians to pray for them. When you are in a crisis, you *want* the elders to help you, because they are on the inside track with the Lord. You want brothers and sisters who have their telephones connected. There is no embarrassment here. These men know not only suffering and joy personally, but they also have a strong and powerful relationship with God. They are your shepherds; they know the power of prayer (James 5:13–15).

David, the shepherd king, was inspired to express it this way:

> The eyes of the Lord are toward the righteous, and His ears are open to their cry. The face of the Lord is against evildoers, to cut off the memory of them from the earth. The righteous cry and the Lord hears, and delivers them out of all their troubles. The Lord is near to the brokenhearted, and saves those who are crushed in spirit (Psalm 34:15–18).

As we close this chapter, let's meditate on a song by David, a song of deliverance and trust in his God:

> I love the Lord, because He hears my voice and my supplications. Because He has inclined His ear to me, therefore I shall call upon

Him as long as I live. The cords of death encompassed me, and the terrors of Sheol came upon me; I found distress and sorrow. Then I called upon the name of the Lord: "O Lord, I beseech Thee, save my life!"

Gracious is the Lord, and righteous; yes, our God is compassionate. The Lord preserves the simple; I was brought low, and He saved me. Return to your rest, O my soul, for the Lord has dealt bountifully with you. For thou hast rescued my soul from death, my eyes from tears, my feet from stumbling. I shall walk before the Lord in the land of the living. I believed when I said, "I am greatly afflicted." I said in my alarm, "All men are liars."

What shall I render to the Lord for all His benefits toward me? I shall lift up the cup of salvation, and call upon the name of the Lord. I shall pay my vows to the Lord, oh, may it be in the presence of all His people. Precious in the sight of the Lord is the death of His godly ones. O Lord, surely I am Thy servant, I am Thy servant, the son of Thy handmaid, Thou hast loosed my bonds. To Thee I shall offer a sacrifice of thanksgiving, and call upon the name of the Lord. I shall pay my vows to the Lord, oh, may it be in the presence of all His people, in the courts of the Lord's house, in the midst of you, O Jerusalem. Praise the Lord! (Psalm 116:1–19).

> "Thou hast rescued my soul from death, my eyes from tears, my feet from stumbling."

## THOUGHTS TO PONDER

1. How does communication help a relationship?

2. Tell of an incident in your life when material things did not bring you the happiness you expected.

3. Why do we ask faithful Christians to pray for us?

4. List the concerns on your heart today; then open your gift of prayer.

5. Define *seek* as used in Psalm 105:3–4.

## SONG FOR TODAY

### HOW LONG HAS IT BEEN?

How long has it been since you talked with the Lord,
And told Him your heart's hidden secrets?
How long since you prayed?
How long since you stayed
On your knees 'til the light shone through?
How long has it been since you woke with the dawn,
And felt that the day's worth the living?

Chorus: Can you call Him your Friend?
How long has it been
Since you knew that He cared for you?

## PRAYER FOR TODAY

*Our Father, we bow before Your throne, giving You all the glory and all the majesty that is Yours. Thank you, O Father, for loving us, for creating us, and for delivering us from sin through Your sweet Son. But most of all, our Father, we thank You for giving us the marvelous gift of prayer—the avenue through which we can seek Your face and tell You what is on our heart. Oh, Father, thank You for You! In Jesus' name. Amen.*

# BECKY'S MEMORIES

## THE LONGEST GOODBYE

Some call Alzheimer's disease "the long goodbye." I have another name for it—"the longest goodbye." Whether the dementia is Alzheimer's or not, I don't know; the telltale signs are there for the family to observe. Constant memory loss, mood swings, vacant stares. The family of the victim can only helplessly watch, often wondering if each farewell is the last one—and there are many "last ones."

It was as if a stranger, a quiet little old lady, came and inhabited my mother's body. She looked at us and smiled sweetly most of the time. But she was like the little girl who "when she was good, she was very, very good, and when she was bad, she was horrid."

When I was a child, Mom often called Daddy "Hoss Cartwright." Remember Hoss from the TV show *Bonanza?* He was big and strong with a gentle heart. Dad was an excellent caregiver, too. He saw to Mom's every need, and I never saw him lose his temper or mistreat her, even though he experienced many times of sheer frustration.

As Mom grew progressively worse, Dad began calling me more frequently in the evening after he had put her to bed. We laughed and cried together; our pain was mutual. We both missed Mom. He once said to me, "What I miss most is talking and reminiscing about our memories. She just is not there."

Sometimes Dad would call and say, "Oh, I had my sweetheart today. She was so good and pleasant. We have had such a good day." And my heart would rejoice because I knew God had given Dad a sweet day with his best girl. And then there were the times that Dad called, and I knew his day had been awful with Mom. But he was always quick to reassure me that he had no regrets in taking care of Mom. He did not want anyone else to care for her.

I cannot describe how absolutely agonizing and desperate it is to watch someone you love so much slip away from you. One of the hardest things for me to accept was that Mom no longer knew me. There were times when she knew I looked familiar, but that was all. We had always had such a close relationship. We were two peas in a pod—"cut from the same cloth," she would often say. However, I am so appreciative of something one of Mom's sweet nurses—an angel—said: "Honey, your mama is in her own world. She is fine. It is you that is hurting." That statement helped me in so many ways then, and it still helps me today.

From the time Mom's macular degenerative eye disease was diagnosed, her dementia progressed rapidly. She could hardly see anything, and her love for studying the Bible, watching TV, and reading was snatched away from her. She seemed to be falling down into a hole, and we could not stop the impending disaster.

I particularly remember a Thanksgiving that my brother Tom and his wife Linda and Jeff and I shared with Mom and Dad at their house. When we had finished with the turkey and the pumpkin pie, Mom suddenly appeared from the back of the house, rushed to me, and grabbed my arm. "Hurry," she said, "someone is in the back of the house! I don't know who he is." I replied quietly, "Mom, it's Daddy. You are all right. He is in his bedroom." With a wild look in her eyes, she kept pleading with me and clinging to my arm. Calming her was no easy task. I had finally experienced one of her hallucinations. They were happening with increasing frequency.

Mom was always funny. Even after she developed dementia she managed some pretty humorous expressions. Thank God for those laughs. "Mom, who am I?" I sometimes said, testing her. She always shot back with gleam in her eye, skillfully avoiding the issue: "Don't you know who you are?"

How could I forget the day we had to take her to the nursing home? After Dad's sudden death, that was our only alternative. I was fixing her a breakfast of cereal and toast when she said, "This is delicious. Who are you?" I told her that I was her daughter Becky. She then asked, "Where do you come from?" She had always told me I came from heaven, so I decided to try a little joke on her: "I come from heaven." She immediately replied, "Get real!"

I laughed: "Don't you think I come from heaven?" She quickly said, "No, I certainly do not!" Mom had frequently told me to please put her in a nursing home when she could not take care of herself. I am very grateful to her for that. There is enough guilt at best in dealing with elderly parents. Leaving her at the nursing home was the hardest thing I have ever done. She was trying to find me; my heart broke to walk away. But I knew I could not care for her properly. She had worn me out in eight days. How in the world did Daddy do it for all those years? God gave him the strength he needed, but he finally just wore out, as caregivers do. God called him home one beautiful April morning.

Now Daddy was gone. I could not talk to Him. Mom was gone, too, in a sense; I could not talk to her. But I could talk to my heavenly Father. He was always there. I needed Him; I needed His comfort and His answers. He never disappointed me.

It was during that nursing home ordeal that I experienced a closeness with God I had never had. It seemed that He was constantly with me, delivering me, and helping me overcome every obstacle. Every prayer was immediately answered and every obstacle dealt with in a positive manner. I could only describe this feeling as if my feet had been covered in oil and I was flying through every door that tried to stop me. Mom had taught me the precious comfort of Deuteronomy 33:26–27:

> There is none like the God of Jeshurun [Israel], who rides the heavens to your help, and through the skies in His majesty. The eternal God is a dwelling place, and underneath are the everlasting arms.

She would say, "Can't you just picture it: God is like Superman—whhshhh! Flying through the air to help us in a crisis, scooping us up and cradling us in His wonderful arms." I read this passage a lot, and I could feel those arms.

I was walking through my den one day, pondering the many obstacles and problems that had suddenly been solved amidst all the sorrow and conflict, when I stopped dead in my tracks. I was listening to an a cappella chorus singing the third verse of "Be with Me, Lord."

> Be with me, Lord! No other gift or blessing
> Thou couldst bestow, could with this one compare—
> A constant sense of Thy abiding presence,
> Where e're I am, to feel that Thou are near.

That was exactly what I was experiencing—a constant sense of God's abiding presence. I truly lived and breathed a beautiful Scripture: "I will never desert you, nor will I ever forsake you" (Hebrews 13:5). I was never alone.

Somehow I knew that God, Jesus, and the Holy Spirit were in charge, and they would help me through this crisis. I never doubted God's love. In fact, I knew His loving arms were wrapped around me; I knew He loved me. All I had to do was pray—talk to Him—and He was there with me. It was the most amazing thing I have ever experienced: so absolutely wonderful, so comforting, so healing.

When I was a little girl, my mother hovered over me when I was sick. She was an excellent nurse. But what I remember most was her pet phrase for any of us kids when we were sick: "Bless your little heart." Traveling this road with my mother and my father certainly brought me to the realization that my sweet Father in heaven was hovering over me, too, saying, "Bless your little heart."

MOM & DAD

CHAPTER 3

# CORNELIUS, A MAN OF PRAYER

Now there was a certain man at Caesarea
named Cornelius, a centurion
of what was called the Italian cohort,
a devout man, and one who feared God
with all his household,
and gave many alms to the Jewish people,
and prayed to God continually
(Acts 10:1-2).

In Acts 10 we find the wonderful conversion story of Cornelius, a commander over one hundred men in the Roman army. The Bible describes Cornelius' excellent qualities:

✠ He was a devout man.

✠ He feared God with all his household.

✠ He gave many alms to the people.

✠ He prayed to God continually—always.

Although His personality traits are outstanding, we must add another important factor to this story: Cornelius was a Gentile. There is no evidence that Cornelius had converted to Judaism. He was a Gentile who believed in and feared Jehovah God. He gave often and generously to people in need—of all races. He had much influence on his family and servants. They, too, feared God.

## A SOLDIER OF ANCIENT VIRTUE

Cornelius was a soldier of the Roman Empire, an empire known for its numerous gods and goddesses. The Romans delighted in their

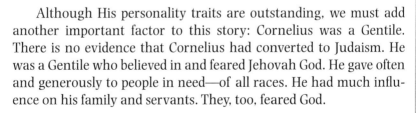

idol worship, but Cornelius prayed to God regularly. How unusual. Where and how was he introduced to Jehovah God? Could it be his path had crossed our Savior's path? Was he the centurion at the cross when Jesus was crucified? Let's look at Matthew, Mark, and Luke's accounts of the centurion at the cross:

- Now the centurion, and those who were with him keeping guard over Jesus, when they saw the earthquake and the things that were happening, became very frightened and said, "Truly this was the Son of God!" (Matthew 27:54).

- And when the centurion, who was standing right in front of Him, saw the way He breathed His last, he said, "Truly this man was the Son of God!" (Mark 15:39).

- Now when the centurion saw what had happened, he began praising God, saying, "Certainly this Man was innocent" (Luke 23:47).

God does not reveal whether or not these men were the same. We will not know the real truth until we get to the other side. Burton Coffman wrote this about Cornelius:

> That the devout Gentile chosen by God for the special treatment accorded him in such things as (1) visitation by an angel, (2) hearing the gospel preached by one of the Twelve, (3) having the Holy Spirit fall upon him in a manifestation suggesting that of Pentecost, etc.—that the Gentile chosen for such blessings should have been a soldier must be regarded as significant . . . There are some eight or ten centurions mentioned in the New Testament, and without exception they all appear in a favorable and commendable light. In the decadent condition of the Roman Empire at that time, the non-commissioned officers of the imperial army constituted something of a residual repository of the ancient virtues of honesty, sobriety, integrity, and the fear of God. Only this could account for the number and character of the centurions mentioned in the New Testament (James Burton Coffman, *Acts* [A.C.U. Press: Abilene, TX, 1975], 197).

## A MEMORIAL OF PRAYERS AND ALMS

By the time we meet Cornelius in Acts 10, some four years have passed since the day of Pentecost and the first gospel sermon preached by Peter in Jerusalem to several thousand Jews. The gospel of Jesus Christ was proclaimed to many cities by their citizens who were visiting in Jerusalem on Pentecost. After that, a great persecution scattered other Christians to many other places.

Cornelius was most likely not a part of the crowd at Pentecost, but God had a plan for him. He heard Cornelius' prayers and saw his generous alms. In fact, it was when Cornelius was praying that He sent an angel to him! (Acts 10:30). Listen to what the angel told Cornelius: "Your prayers and alms have ascended as a memorial before God" (Acts 10:4).

> What interest attaches to these words! Man's natural desire for a permanent memorial may truly be realized, but not in the types of monuments so often erected. The true memorial ascends to the presence of the Father in heaven, and it is made up of the prayers and alms of those who, upon earth, loved God and sought to know and do his will (Coffman, *Acts*, 200).

Cornelius proved by his deeds that he had a good heart and wanted to please God. His prayers and benevolent acts reached the throne room of God. Luke describes Cornelius as praying always. God knows about sincere people who are constantly in prayer to Him.

## PRAYER IS NOT ENOUGH

Praying to God and helping the needy were not enough to get Cornelius to heaven. If so, his story would have ended right there. Surely those who hold to the doctrine that praying to God is enough for salvation dare not read the story of Cornelius. And surely those who cater to the idea that belief in God is all one needs in order to go to heaven would be completely rebuffed with this account of the centurion from Caesarea. It does not take a rocket scientist to see that if a person prays continually to Jehovah God, he believes in Jehovah God. But belief is not enough. If it were, then why did God send Peter to teach Cornelius? Was not James, the brother of Christ, inspired to write in James 2:19: "You believe that God is one. You do well; the demons also believe, and shudder"? Are these demons saved or lost? They are still lost.

> Praying to God and helping the needy were not enough to get Cornelius to heaven.

I have heard some teach that God does not hear the prayers of sinners. Well, I believe the case of Cornelius completely refutes that notion! The angel's words verify this: "Your prayers and alms have ascended." God certainly heard the constant praying of this soldier. When Luke describes Cornelius' acts, the act of praying continually is listed last. But it is Cornelius' prayers that the angel mentions first—and then the alms. Interesting, don't you think?

> God's plan for Gentiles to be a part of His church was not a last-minute idea.

Jehovah heard the prayers of Cornelius and saw his good works. God has always loved men and women who loved Him, whether Jew or Gentile. The time had arrived for the Gentiles to come into the church for which Jesus died, and Cornelius was honored by being the very first.

God's plan for Gentiles to be a part of His church was not a last-minute idea. In that first gospel sermon on the day of Pentecost, Peter said,

> Repent, and let each of you be baptized in the name of Jesus Christ for the forgiveness of your sins; and you shall receive the gift of the Holy Spirit. For the promise is for you and your children, and for all who are far off, as many as the Lord our God shall call to Himself (Acts 2:38–39).

## SALVATION'S DOOR OPENS TO THE GENTILES

The Gentiles were those who were "far off." "But now in Christ Jesus you who formerly were far off have been brought near by the blood of Christ" (Ephesians 2:13). "And He came and preached peace to you who were far away, and peace to those who were near" (Ephesians 2:17).

Read the account in Acts 10 and see how God magnificently coordinated Peter's vision on the rooftop and the visit of three men sent from Cornelius. When Peter arrived at Cornelius' home, Cornelius had gathered his entire household, relatives, and friends to hear Peter's message from God. Once again we see the good heart of Cornelius and his desire to know God's will for him. He must have been an evangelist at heart. Cornelius had been doing some door knocking!

Peter, a common fisherman, had been honored by Jesus in Matthew 16. When Jesus asked His disciples, "Who do people say that the Son of Man is," it was Peter who demonstrated great knowledge and faith: "Thou art the Christ, the Son of the living God." Christ then said to him,

> Blessed are you, Simon Barjona, because flesh and blood did not reveal this to you, but My Father who is in heaven. And I also say to you that you are Peter, and upon this rock I will build My church; and the gates of Hades shall not overpower it. I will give you the keys of the kingdom of heaven; and whatever you shall bind on earth shall have been bound in heaven, and whatever you shall loose on earth shall have been loosed in heaven (Matthew 16:17–19 NASU).

What were the keys of the kingdom? Peter was to have the express honor of preaching the first gospel sermon to open the doors of the church of Christ. Christ's kingdom, the church, was established on the day of Pentecost. The three thousand baptized that day were added to the church.

Later Peter used the keys of the kingdom in preaching the gospel of Jesus Christ in Caesarea. He preached the same message, but this time these keys were used to open the door of salvation to the Gentiles.

Cornelius was willing to do anything God asked of him. He told Peter, "Now then, we are all here present before God to hear all that you have been commanded by the Lord" (Acts 10:33). The Holy Spirit fell on the audience, a sign from God that the Gentiles were to be a part of the kingdom of God.

> While Peter was still speaking these words, the Holy Spirit fell upon all those who were listening to the message. And all the circumcised believers who had come with Peter were amazed, because the gift of the Holy Spirit had been poured out upon the Gentiles also. For they were hearing them speaking with tongues and exalting God. Then Peter answered, "Surely no one can refuse the water for these to be baptized who have received the Holy Spirit just as we did, can he?" And he ordered them to be baptized in the name of Jesus Christ. Then they asked him to stay on for a few days (Acts 10:44–48).

## ACTION SPRINGS FROM WILLING HEARTS

Both Cornelius and the Ethiopian eunuch of Acts 8 had willing hearts—hearts that wanted to please God in all things. When they heard the gospel of Jesus Christ, their response was immediate; they obeyed God. Their hearts were right. It is easy to imagine the joy and happiness that occurred when their conversions took place. The Bible says of the conversion of the eunuch: "And when they came up out of the water, the Spirit of the Lord snatched Philip away; and the eunuch saw him no more, but went on his way rejoicing" (Acts 8:39).

The gospel of Jesus Christ demands action. And that action is doing whatever Jesus has commanded. Cornelius and the Ethiopian eunuch had no problem with obedience. Just what has Jesus commanded us to do?

✠ If you love Me, you will keep My commandments (John 14:15).

✠ I said therefore to you, that you shall die in your sins; for unless you believe that I am He, you shall die in your sins (John 8:24).

✠ Everyone therefore who shall confess Me before men, I will also confess him before My Father who is in heaven (Matthew 10:32).

✠ I tell you, no, but unless you repent, you will all likewise perish (Luke 13:3).

✠ He who has believed and has been baptized shall be saved; but he who has disbelieved shall be condemned (Mark 16:16).

✠ Not everyone who says to Me, "Lord, Lord," will enter the kingdom of heaven; but he who does the will of My Father who is in heaven (Matthew 7:21).

And what are the end results of His commands? Forgiveness. Pure joy and pure salvation.

## SEARCH! GOD WILL SEND A TEACHER

Are there other lessons to be learned from the story of Cornelius? Yes! When one is searching for the truth, God will send him a teacher. The Creator knows our hearts; nothing is hidden from Him.

While being raised in the mission field, I heard countless stories of men and women who wanted to find a church that studied only the Bible. No creeds. No doctrines of men. Just the word of God. Each seeker had a "love story," we called them. Simply told, these love stories were accounts of how God helped them to find the truth. Many times it was a matter of a person simply walking into the church building with a ton of questions. Other times it was a friend or a chance encounter that resulted in a Bible study. Nancy, a dear sister in Connecticut, was once an actress. She and a fellow actor studied the Bible as their touring group traveled to theaters to perform. One day in desperation Nancy opened up the huge phone book and chose a church. That church taught the gospel of Jesus Christ.

> "And you will seek Me and find Me, when you search for Me with all your heart."

I never tire of hearing these stories. They are beautiful, phenomenal accounts of God's hands at work in people's lives, people who wanted to find God. And God heard and answered their cries and pleas for help.

Two powerful passages from Psalms and Jeremiah give hope to those who pray:

> Come and hear, all who fear God, and I will tell of what He has done for my soul. I cried to Him with my mouth, and He was extolled with my tongue. If I regard wickedness in my heart, the Lord will not hear; but certainly God has heard; He has given heed to the voice of my prayer. Blessed be God, who has not turned away my prayer, nor His lovingkindness from me (Psalm 66:16–20).

> "For I know the plans that I have for you," declares the Lord, "plans for welfare and not for calamity to give you a future and a hope. Then you will call upon Me and come and pray to Me, and I will listen to you. And you will seek Me and find Me, when you search for Me with all your heart" (Jeremiah 29:11–13).

## THE FOOLISHNESS OF PREACHING

There is yet another lesson in the story of Cornelius. Who brought the gospel to Cornelius and his household? An angel? No. Angels never taught the gospel to any man or woman in the Scriptures. That is not their job. Coffman says that these holy beings aid "providentially in bringing sinners into contact with the gospel" (Coffman, *Acts*, 200).

God has seen fit to give people the task of teaching other people. One preacher put it this way: "The goal of every Christian is another Christian." The gospel has been given into our hands, and what we do with it is crucial. We can either ignore it or share it. To keep it to ourselves is wrong. God never intended the gospel to be exclusively taught to just one group of people, as He is no respecter of persons (Acts 10:34). Cornelius is evidence of this, isn't he?

> But we have this treasure in earthen vessels, that the surpassing greatness of the power may be of God and not from ourselves; we are afflicted in every way, but not crushed; perplexed, but not despairing; persecuted, but not forsaken; struck down, but not destroyed; always carrying about in the body the dying of Jesus, that the life of Jesus also may be manifested in our body (2 Corinthians 4:7–10).

The gospel is the treasure that we carry, and the earthen vessel is our body that holds the gospel. We are God's messengers, too, and it is our job to share this gospel with the world. If our bodies are to manifest the life of Jesus Christ, then we must remind ourselves of Jesus' words:

> You are the light of the world. A city set on a hill cannot be hidden. Nor do men light a lamp, and put it under the peck-measure, but on the lampstand; and it gives light to all who are in the house. Let your light shine before men in such a way that they may see your good works, and glorify your Father who is in heaven (Matthew 5:14–16).

## GROUND ZERO

Romans 1:16 says the gospel is the power of God. The Greek word for power is *dunamis*, the root word for dynamite. I like to think of the day of Pentecost as being "Ground Zero," the beginning of Christianity. We can certainly say that the gospel was the dynamite that exploded in Jerusalem that day. That dynamite gospel exploded again at the home of Cornelius. Nothing would ever be the same again. As the gospel of Jesus Christ changed lives that day, it continues to change lives today.

Brother Marshall Keeble was a powerful preacher known for his "down to earth" humor. Note his comments about the gospel:

> You can't set a hen on a brown leghorn's eggs and expect white leghorn chickens. Neither can you plant man-made doctrine in the hearts of men and women and expect Christians. The Word of God—the gospel—is the seed of the kingdom, and it will produce Christians every time, but that's all it will produce! The gospel has power, great power. All it needs is someone to preach it—someone with courage to tell it just like it is" (Willie Cato, *His Hand and Heart* [J. C. Choate Publications: Winona/Singapore/New Dehli, 1990], 39).

The gospel is the treasure that we carry, and the earthen vessel is our body that holds the gospel.

The story of Cornelius is the story of us. We are Gentiles, as Cornelius was. And we are now soldiers, as Cornelius was. The gospel, the good news of Jesus, is for all people. There is no discrimination with God; all are welcome.

> How then shall they call upon Him in whom they have not believed? And how shall they believe in Him whom they have not heard? And how shall they hear without a preacher? And how shall they preach unless they are sent? Just as it is written, "How beautiful are the feet of those who bring glad tidings of good things!" (Romans 10:14–15).

Of all people, we should be the most thankful. Now we have an obligation to carry the gospel everywhere we go.

The book of Matthew closes with the *Great Commission*. It is as applicable today as it was two thousand years ago. We must go. We must baptize. We must teach. That is our mission until the Lord calls us home:

> All authority has been given to Me in heaven and on earth. Go therefore and make disciples of all the nations, baptizing them in the name of the Father and the Son and the Holy Spirit, teaching them to observe all that I commanded you; and lo, I am with you always, even to the end of the age (Matthew 28:18–20).

## THOUGHTS TO PONDER

1. List the attributes of Cornelius.

2. Who did God send first to Cornelius?

3. What were the "keys of the kingdom"?

4. What is the treasure that earthen vessels hold?

## SONG FOR TODAY

### INTO OUR HANDS

Swiftly we're turning life's daily pages,
Swiftly the hours are changing to years;
How are we using God's golden moments?
Shall we reap glory? Shall we reap tears?

Millions are groping without the gospel,
Quickly they'll reach eternity's night;
Shall we sit idly as they rush onward?
Haste, let us hold up Christ the true light.

Souls that are precious, souls that are dying,
While we rejoice our sins are forgiv'n;
Did He not also die for these lost ones?
Then let us point the way unto heav'n.

Chorus: Into our hands the gospel is given,
Into our hands is given the light,
Haste, let us carry God's precious message,
Guiding the erring back to the right.

## PRAYER FOR TODAY

*Dear Father in heaven, thank You for this marvelous story of Cornelius. Thank You for loving the Gentiles enough to allow them to hear the gospel, obey the gospel, and have a home with You someday. Thank You for hearing this Gentile soldier's prayer. Thank You for your generous mercy, love, and grace that You now extend to us. Please help us all to be faithful soldiers in Your army. We love You, Father. In Jesus' name. Amen.*

# BECKY'S MEMORIES
## FIRST LOVE NOT BEST LOVE

If you are a parent of a teenager, remember that you were once a teen. More than one girl has told me, "I don't know what to do. I have asked Mom what she did about this when she was my age. She told me she didn't remember being my age!" Oh, yes, that mama does remember. She just does not want to be bothered. Or she doesn't want to be reminded of her own mistakes!

When our daughter was a teen, we had great difficulty with her choice of a boyfriend, particularly his dress. I was at my parents' home letting off steam when my mother kindly asked, "Becky, don't you remember how long Terry's hair was?"

How do mothers have instant recall of unfortunate situations that happened to you so many years ago? I sat there with my mouth open for at least a minute, trying to think of a profound retort, but there was none. At last I nodded my head and swallowed. Then we all burst out laughing. Oh, if we could only learn to laugh about our past, because history just might repeat itself.

When I was in college, I fell in love with the wrong boy. He was wrong for me in every way possible, especially spiritually. He was raised in another religion and was just as adamant about his beliefs as I was about mine. I refused to break the relationship. Needless to say, my parents were very upset with me and with the entire relationship. When I came home for summer vacation, the barometric pressure in our house was palpable. We were at war with each other. That was very unusual because our home was always cheery and lighthearted.

One morning my mother remarked: "Becky, your daddy prayed for you all night long." I looked at her in complete surprise. "He was on his knees all night, praying just for you."

I thought a lot that day about what she had told me. First of all, I realized that my parents were very concerned about the poor decisions I was making. Second, I realized how much they loved me—enough to pray all night long! Third, I realized how wrong I was to torture them so. They loved me and my soul, and they didn't want me to be lost. And fourth, I loved my parents with all my heart. If I married this young man, I stood a very good chance of losing my faith, my soul, and the close relationship I had always had with my parents. They did not deserve this.

The young man was very strong, and I loved him. But my parents' faith in God and His power were stronger. My parents went to the Begging Place several times that summer in my behalf. By summer's end, the romance was over. God delivered all of us. Thank you, my Father, for your infinite wisdom and mercy.

What about you, my friend? Have you ever loved the wrong person?

Chapter 4

# Let's Talk about Prayer

Ask, and it shall be given to you; seek, and you shall find; knock, and it shall be opened to you (Matthew 7:7).

"While Jesus was praying in a certain place, after He had finished, one of His disciples said to Him, 'Lord, teach us to pray' " (Luke 11:1). Where is the first occurrence in the Bible of the word *pray*, the word that means to beseech, to ask, to entreat, to make supplication? Be careful: the King James Version uses "pray" frequently, but it does not always mean going to God in prayer. *Pray*, meaning "to beseech," is first used in Genesis 20:7. God had visited Abimelech in a dream and told him not to touch Sarah. God said,

> Now therefore restore the man's wife, for he is a prophet, and he will pray for you, and you will live . . . And Abraham prayed to God; and God healed Abimelech and his wife and his maids, so that they bore children (Genesis 20:7–17).

Let's look at some definitions of *prayer*:

- A reverent petition made to God, a god, or another object of worship.
- The act of making a reverent petition to God, a god, or another object of worship.
- An act of communion with God, a god, or another object of worship, such as in devotion, confession, praise, or thanksgiving.
- A specially worded form used to address God, a god, or another object of worship.
- A fervent request. (Her prayer for rain was granted at last).

## HOW DO I PRAY?

Am I praying correctly? Is God listening to me? Women desire to pray "in Spirit and truth." We want to please God in our supplications to Him. We want God to listen to us! We make the same plea David made: "Give ear to my prayer, O God; and do not hide Thyself from my supplication" (Psalm 55:1).

Even Christ's closest disciples asked Him how to pray. Evidently they had trouble when praying, too. They must have been listening to Jesus when He prayed. On several occasions Jesus addressed the manner in which we should pray. Keep in mind that the manner in which we do something involves the why, the where, and the how.

> We want to please God in our supplications . . . We want God to listen to us!

Let's look at Luke 11:1–13 (NKJV) and see what God is telling us. (Compare this account with Matthew 6:9–13):

*Now it came to pass, as He was praying in a certain place, when He ceased, that one of His disciples said to Him, "Lord, teach us to pray, as John also taught his disciples."*

- ◆ Jesus was accustomed to praying wherever He traveled, and a disciple decided to take this opportunity to ask Him a question that was on his mind.

- ◆ John the Baptist taught his followers how to pray. These disciples wanted to pray correctly, too, just like Jesus' disciples wanted. Somehow this particular disciple of Jesus knew what went on in the "John the Baptist" camp. Could it be that he had been a disciple of John?

*So He said to them, "When you pray, say: Our Father in heaven."*

- ◆ When we pray, the very first thing we must acknowledge is that God is our Father. He is the majestic Maker and Creator of all, but He alone is our Father. We are His children; we can have a close and intimate relationship with Him.

- ◆ We pray to the Father and not to anyone else.

*"Hallowed be Your name."*

◆ God is holy and to be revered.

◆ The name of God is sacred.

*"Your kingdom come."*

◆ The church was going to be established. Today we pray for the kingdom to prosper, not "to come." It was established on Pentecost (Acts 2).

◆ Christ is ready for His bride.

*"Your will be done on earth as it is in heaven."*

◆ Lord, we want Your will to be done at all cost. Not our will.

◆ You rule heaven and earth.

*"Give us day by day our daily bread."*

◆ The Lord has always provided the food we need every day of our lives. Remember the manna in the wilderness?

◆ Note "this day" and "daily." Today is all you have. Don't ask for tomorrow's bread.

*"And forgive us our sins, for we also forgive everyone who is indebted to us."*

◆ God the Father has the power to forgive our transgressions.

◆ We know how sinful we are, and we know that we must forgive those who sin against us. God is merciful to us, and we, in turn, must show mercy to those who hurt us.

*"And do not lead us into temptation."*

◆ Please help us not to sin or be tempted to sin.

◆ Help us to recognize evil.

*"But deliver us from the evil one."*

◆ Satan is alive and well.

◆ Deliver us from him.

*"Which of you shall have a friend, and go to him at midnight and say to him, 'Friend, lend me three loaves; for a friend of mine has come to me on his journey, and I have nothing to set before him'; and he will answer from within and say, 'Do not trouble me; the door is now shut, and my children*

*are with me in bed: I cannot rise and give to you'? I say to you, though he will not rise and give to him because he is his friend, yet because of his persistence he will rise and give him as many as he needs"* (Luke 11:5–8 NKJV).

- ◆ God teaches us not only persistence, but also courage and bravery when we seek Him in prayer.

- ◆ We are not to be afraid of Him or of talking to Him.

- ◆ Our hearts' desires are to be poured out to the Father, because they are as urgent to us as if we had no food in the house, and a hungry mouth was at our door.

- ◆ Our persistence and our courage will bring results. Someone once said, "Though unpretentious and often unheard by men, prayer is one of the mightiest weapons God has placed in our hands."

*"So I say to you, ask, and it will be given to you; seek, and you will find; knock, and it will be opened to you. For everyone who asks receives, and he who seeks finds, and to him who knocks it will be opened"* (Luke 11:9–10 NKJV).

- ◆ Try to remember it this way:

  A—Ask

  S—Seek

  K—Knock

- ◆ Pray, pray, and pray. God is listening. He will answer your prayer.

## ACTS

"Acts" is a way of remembering the basic elements of prayer. Keep this acrostic in mind when praying:

A—adoration of God and acknowledgment that He is God

C—confess your sins

T—thanksgiving

S—self, supplication

## PRAYER IS THE BIRTHPLACE OF FAITH

Solomon was inspired to say in Ecclesiastes, "There is nothing new under the sun." How true! People today are the same as they were three thousand years ago. We face the same fundamental temptations. We pursue wealth only to discover that the wealthy have a new set of problems. During the first half of our lives we spend our health pursuing wealth; during the last half of our lives we spend our wealth pursuing health.

Are we like that disciple in Luke 11? We want to pray right, but we know we are unworthy sinners. For us to come to the throne of God with a request is not a small matter. Our prayer life is the power connection in our relationship with the Lord.

James tells us how effective our prayers can be: We don't have because we don't ask! (James 4:2). It takes faith on our part to ask God to do His part. What a comfort to know that when we pray, God will not be hearing any surprise requests or sudden transgressions. As the omniscient one, God already knows our hearts. He already knows what we are going to say, even before the words are on our lips. He already knows what sins we have committed. And He already knows how He is going to answer our prayer.

*"Even before there is a word on my tongue, behold, O Lord, Thou dost know it all."*

> O Lord, Thou hast searched me and known me, Thou dost know when I sit down and when I rise up; Thou dost understand my thought from afar. Thou dost scrutinize my path and my lying down, and art intimately acquainted with all my ways. Even before there is a word on my tongue, behold, O Lord, Thou dost know it all (Psalm 139:1–4).

## PRAYER IS THE BIRTHPLACE OF OUR JOURNEY

Through prayer we learn to "let go and let God," and that is called trust. In prayer we mentally surrender ourselves to His will—whatever that will is. We, too, must pray as Jesus did in the Garden of Gethsemane: "Yet not My will, but Thine be done" (Luke 22:42).

Accepting God's will for our lives and not fighting Him tooth and nail over every little matter that concerns us brings peace into our turbulent lives. Praying that His will be done instead of ours bestows relief and respite. At the end of the day, don't we all want peace?

Read Psalm 4, and focus on verses 1, 3, 4, 5, and 8:

> Answer me when I call, O God, of my righteousness! Thou has relieved me in my distress; be gracious to me and hear my prayer . . . But know that the Lord has set apart the godly man for Himself; the Lord hears when I call to Him. Tremble, and do not sin; meditate in your heart upon your bed, and be still. Offer the sacrifices of righteousness, and trust in the Lord . . . In peace I will both lie down and sleep, for Thou alone, O Lord, dost make me to dwell in safety (Psalm 4:1–8).

How beautiful! Don't you love the words, "meditate in your heart"? What a perfect description of prayer. When we pray, we meditate in our heart. We quietly think about what is on our heart—sometimes passionately—and offer it to the Lord.

## PRAYER IS THE BIRTHPLACE OF LOVE

As we see God's answering our prayers and solving our problems, we sink to our knees in gratitude for His mercy. Our love for our Father grows. As our love grows, we develop into more mature Christians. Our relationship with God continues to grow. We find ourselves seeking God more and more and praying more and more, because we realize He has all the answers and we have none. Our trust in Him increases as we see His hand working out our problems.

Finally, we arrive at this most profound conclusion: the Christian life is the best way to live, and prayer is the key! The journey is not so difficult when God is by our side hearing and answering our prayers, delivering us and maturing us into good, obedient children. Someone wisely said, "More things are wrought by prayer than this world dreams of." And sometimes good and obedient children will suffer discipline or spankings from the Lord. Yes, we even learn from His discipline that He loves us. The following verses affirm it:

> My son, do not regard lightly the discipline of the Lord, nor faint when you are reproved by Him; for those whom the Lord loves He disciplines, and He scourges every son whom He receives . . . Furthermore, we had earthly fathers to discipline us, and we respected them; shall we not much rather be subject to the Father of spirits,

and live? For they disciplined us for a short time as seemed best to them, but He disciplines us for our good, that we may share His holiness (Hebrews 12:5–10).

Behold, how happy is the man whom God reproves, so do not despise the discipline of the Almighty (Job 5:17).

My son, do not reject the discipline of the Lord, or loathe His reproof, for whom the Lord loves He reproves, even as a father, the son in whom he delights (Proverbs 3:11–12).

If God did not love us, He would not care one whit about making us obedient children. But He does love us; therefore, we will experience reprimands by our Father. It will not be pleasant, but it will yield a better us. Just as chastening our own children makes them better, God's corrections help us to be upright and more attentive to His will. This is surrender all over again.

> We must see every affliction as allotted to us by our heavenly Father, and in it we must discover His correcting hand. Therefore, we must wait on Him to know the reason why He contends with us, the fault for which He chastens us, the bad attitude that needs to be cured in us. Then we can fulfill God's purpose in afflicting us and so be made partakers of His holiness. We must watch the motions of Providence, we must keep our eyes upon our Father when He frowns, so that we may discover what His mind is and what the obedience is that we are to learn by the things that we suffer (Hebrews 5:8) (Henry, *Experiencing God's Presence*, 89–90).

> If God did not love us, He would not care one whit about making us obedient children.

How true! When we are experiencing God's hand of correction or going through trying times, the Bible contains the antidote. David concluded that discipline from God was good for him because it made him turn to God's Word: "It is good for me that I was afflicted, that I may learn Thy statutes. The law of Thy mouth is better to me than thousands of gold and silver pieces" (Psalm 119:71–72).

## HEAVENLY DISCIPLINE

The proverb says, "Correct your son, and he will give you rest" (Proverbs 29:17 NKJV). What does that mean? Well, children can drive you crazy if you let them. They will pester and harass you; they will make constant noise until you surrender to their desires. But God tells us to discipline them. Don't give in to them. Teach them and rebuke them. What will be the final result? Rest and peace in the home. There is quiet again—and normalcy. Storms of selfishness and persistent gratification disappear because a parent said that is enough and then administered the "board of education." Peace, sweet peace reigns supreme in the home now. The child is at peace, and so is the parent.

> They will pester and harass you; they will make constant noise until you surrender to their desires.

The same is true of God's children. We clamor for His attention to our needs (or wants) and demand that He change our lives. We may be forty years old, behaving like a stubborn teenager. However, we need to realize He is already working in our lives; He knows what is best for us, despite our whiney ways. He knows how to use problems and trials to direct our focus back on Him. That is the Father's way of spanking His children. The result is peace in our lives, along with a healthy dose of respect and adoration for Him.

## ANXIETY ATTACKS

I have heard my mother say when speaking to Christian sisters: "Have you ever stopped to think that even anxiety attacks could be from God? He is trying to say to us, 'Have you checked in with Me yet?'"

Let us not forget the passage we just read in Hebrews 12:10. God's plan in disciplining us is to yield what in our lives? Holiness. God desires that we share in His holiness. The root word of *holiness* is *holy*. According to the *New World Dictionary*, *holy* has several meanings: belonging to God, consecrated, sacred, spiritually pure; untainted by evil or sin.

When we are baptized, we become new creatures. We have killed the old self—I call her the "old girl." This new girl no longer lives for herself. She is dedicated and committed to God; He is now number one in her life. She no longer walks as she used to walk, because she has chosen an entirely different and new path on which to travel. Paul was inspired to say it this way:

> That, in reference to your former manner of life, you lay aside the old self, which is being corrupted in accordance with the lusts of deceit, and that you be renewed in the spirit of your mind, and put on the new self, which in the likeness of God has been created in righteousness and holiness of the truth (Ephesians 4:22–24).

> Therefore be imitators of God, as beloved children (Ephesians 5:1).

prayer is the key to heaven, but faith unlocks the door.

## WORRY OR PRAY?

Worry? Why worry?
What can worry do?
It never keeps a trouble from overtaking you.
It gives you indigestion and sleepless hours at night
And fills with gloom the days, however fair and bright.
It puts a frown upon your face, and sharpness in the tone.
We're unfit to live with others and unfit to live alone;
Worry? Why worry?
What can worry do?
It never keeps a trouble from overtaking you!

Pray? Why pray?
What can praying do?
Praying really changes things, arranges life anew.
It's good for your digestion, gives you peaceful sleep at night
And fills the grayest, gloomiest day with rays of glowing light.
It puts a smile upon your face, the love note in your tone,
Makes you fit to live with others, and fit to live alone.
Pray? Why pray?
What can praying do?
It brings God down from heaven, to live and work with you!

    —Anonymous

## HOLY BEHAVIOR

I heard a preacher say: "God has just one goal for His children. He just wants them to look like Him." I agree, and holiness is what our Father in heaven looks like.

This "holiness" concept is hard for old Becky to grasp. There is no way I can be holy like God—it simply is too unfathomable. But this concept is not hard for God to grasp. Listen to the words of the apostle Peter, being inspired by the Holy Spirit:

> As obedient children, do not be conformed to the former lusts which were yours in your ignorance, but like the Holy One who called you, be holy yourselves also in all your behavior; because it is written, "You shall be holy, for I am holy" (1 Peter 1:14–16).

*If He says we shall be holy, then we shall be. Are we going to argue with the Almighty?*

Surely, if our kind and compassionate Father says we can be holy because He is holy, then He must know what He is talking about. We will trust Him to accomplish holiness in our lives. If He says we shall be holy, then we shall be. Are we going to argue with the Almighty? No sir, not I! I love and adore belonging to Him. God's love is more than enough for me. I am just going to have to trust Him in this "being holy" business. He knows what He is doing.

### THOUGHTS TO PONDER

1. Who asked Jesus for instructions about how to pray?

2. What word can be used as an acrostic for prayer?

3. How do our prayers relate to God's omniscience?

4. Why does God discipline His children?

## SONG FOR TODAY

### SWEET HOUR OF PRAYER

Sweet hour of prayer! Sweet hour of prayer,
That calls me from a world of care,
And bids me at my Father's throne
Make all my wants and wishes known;
In seasons of distress and grief
My soul has often found relief,
And oft escaped the tempter's snare,
By thy return, sweet hour of prayer.

Sweet hour of prayer! Sweet hour of prayer,
The joy I feel, the bliss I share
Of those whose anxious spirits burn
With strong desires for thy return!
With such I hasten to the place
Where God, my Savior, shows His face,
And gladly take my station there,
And wait for thee, sweet hour of prayer.

Sweet hour of prayer! Sweet hour of prayer,
Thy wings shall my petition bear
To Him whose truth and faithfulness
Engage the waiting soul to bless;
And since He bids me seek His face,
Believe His word, and trust His grace,
I'll cast on Him my ev'ry care,
And wait for thee, sweet hour of prayer.

## PRAYER FOR TODAY

*Dear Father, we bow before You and acknowledge Your greatness, Your love, Your compassion, and Your mercy. With Your mighty hand, You created this world and formed our substance. You loved us before we were even here on this earth, and You continue to work in our lives, daily answering our many supplications. It is impossible for us to imagine our lives without You in them. Thank You, O God, for loving us in spite of our faults and flaws. We confess our sins to You. And Lord, we even thank You for chastising us and disciplining us. Please don't give up on us. We are Your children, Your daughters, and we rejoice that You are our kind Father. In Jesus' name. Amen.*

# BECKY'S MEMORIES

## IT'S CANCER!

Are you ever prepared for a sudden catastrophe that flies out of left field and confronts you head-on? Whether a trip to the emergency room with a bleeding child, a dangerous car wreck, the death of a loved one, or infidelity, you try to act calm, composed, Christ-like, and "together." And sometimes you succeed. This is called "test day."

Many times the test is small, and many times it is huge. You are never warned ahead of time. (Wouldn't it be wonderful if you were?) You wake up one morning, feeling great and energetic, not knowing that today will be a day you will never forget. This day may go down in your biography as "the day your life stood still."

Go back with me to May 1977. I was pregnant with our second child—about eight months. Being fair skinned, it is easy to notice anything new or of a different color on my body. I noticed the mole on my left forearm had suddenly changed color. I had my OB/GYN look at it. "There is no cause for alarm," he assured me. "It's simple to remove."

The next week he called: "Becky, this is Dr. Leyva. We have received the lab report on that mole we removed from your arm. It has come back malignant. This is melanoma." I was too stunned to answer.

"Becky, malignant means that this is cancer. Do you understand what I am saying?"

"Yes. Yes I do."

"Do you have a surgeon?"

"No, I don't," I said softly. Then I thought, *I am twenty-nine years old—why would I have a surgeon?*

"Well, I have one for you. I have made an appointment for you at 8:30 tomorrow morning. We must remove more tissue. No doctor wants to operate on a pregnant woman because surgery sometimes induces premature labor. But we must operate. We must make sure we have removed all the cancer. Okay?"

"Okay."

Jeff, my husband, had been listening. We both went into shock, I think. But Jeff managed to go to work, and I proceeded to take care of 19-month-old Jennifer. I moved around the house like a robot.

Mom was always a rock, but she fell apart when I called her. Mom told me later that she hung up the phone and promptly threw herself at the feet of God and started screaming over and over: "Oh, God, no! Please no!" She wept and cried and wailed. She begged and she pleaded. Mom was at the Begging Place.

After several hours, she called me back. She and Dad had called one of their Christian friends, a doctor. He calmed their fears, telling them I was right to have had the mole removed. (Mom and Dad were of the old school: never touch a mole.)

The rock was back. She was Mom again. She stood firm, reassuring me of God's love, protection, and deliverance. I needed all the encouraging words I could get. I felt a calmness in my heart and in my soul; I knew God was alive and well, delivering me and my baby. The Comforter was beside me.

Mom had a favorite Scripture, and she quoted it over and over as I grew up under her wing: "And we know that God causes all things to work together for good to those who love God, to those who are called according to His purpose" (Romans 8:28). When troubles and trials came upon us, she would say, "Well, it's not too much for God. He will make all of this work together for our good. Just wait and see!" And He always did.

In the process of scheduling my surgery, an odd moment occurred in the surgeon's office. My husband asked, "What if Becky had not had that mole removed?"

The surgeon replied tersely: "Then she would have lived about a year." Special prayers were offered at all church meetings.

The surgeon took a wedge of skin from my arm. No plastic surgery. It was too risky. The stitches held the incision together just fine. My arm still has an odd-looking gap on it.

One month later Jeffrey Allen Blackmon, Jr. was born. A total delight—and a total challenge! (Most boys are.) When he has a birthday, I have one too—inside my head. After giving birth to Jeffrey, I was looking out the window as Jeff exited the building. Jeff had told me our little Jennifer was down there. Yes, there she was in her little green, gingham checked dress! I prayed, "Oh, thank You, God, for sparing my life. She needs me, and I need her. I am her mother; I need to raise her."

Through the years there have been special moments when I have observed Jeff, Jennifer, and Jeffrey laughing and having fun together. I watch them from afar. And I am out of the picture. It is a strange feeling. And I think to myself, *This is how it would have been had I died. Just those three—without me.* And then I go to the Begging Place and thank God for my life and for His hearing all those prayers that went up in my behalf. Especially the cries of my mother.

"God tests the righteous and the wicked" (Psalm 11:5). His tests are designed to make us stronger as we turn to Him for help. Satan also tests us—with temptations. His goal is to cause us to sin and turn away from God.

James, the brother of our Lord, wrote a beautiful letter to those scattered by Roman persecution. However, this letter is also written to us. We also undergo tests and trials every day that we live.

> Consider it all joy, my brethren, when you encounter various trials, knowing that the testing of your faith produces endurance. And let endurance have its perfect result, that you may be perfect and complete, lacking in nothing. But if any of you lacks wisdom, let him ask of God, who gives to all men generously and without reproach, and it will be given to him. But let him ask in faith without any doubting, for the one who doubts is like the surf of the sea driven and tossed by the wind. For let not that man expect that he will receive anything from the Lord (James 1:2–7).

God's goal for us is that we grow up. When He tests us, He is teaching us to endure and mature. When the test is over, we will be lacking in absolutely nothing. Why? Because we have learned the lesson—whatever God was trying to teach us—and we have reached another spiritual plateau of the Christian life. Our journey and walk with Him has turned another corner.

When we look back on "test day," we see that it has had its good results in our lives. Even if the test day has brought death or some horrific ordeal, we can eventually see God's hand, not only delivering us but keeping us steady as the storm passed. We realize we had to travel this road and encounter this test. As much as we wanted to, we could not stop this test. We had to see it through, and this, too, is good for us. Trust is what God is teaching His children in these times. Oh, if we would only learn to let go and stop trying to fix the problem! If we would only stop worrying about the outcome and being in control, we would know the power and love of our Father.

The following verses will help in times of testing:

"God is our refuge and strength, a very present help in trouble" (Psalm 46:1).

"Be still, and know that I am God" (Psalm 46:10 NKJV).

If you are a new Christian, do not be discouraged. God is with you, delivering you, and guiding you on your way home. Pray at all times. Stand firm. Don't look back.

If you are an older Christian, you already can recall the many times God has powerfully answered your prayers. Perhaps you have a scar or a gap—something that visibly shows the world God loves you. A wise person once said, "When we get to heaven, God is not going to be looking for all our trophies and prizes we won on earth. He will be looking for the scars and the worn knees that prove we were dedicated Christians." Be proud of your "mark." It is a sign of God's marvelous mercy and God's wondrous love. But most of all, your scar is a sign of God's deliverance and an answered prayer from the Begging Place.

JEFF AND BECKY BLACKMON

CHAPTER 5

# THE PRAYER OF ONE WOMAN— A STORY OF HOPE

She [Hannah], greatly distressed, prayed to the Lord
and wept bitterly. She made a vow and said,
"O Lord of hosts, if You will indeed look on the
affliction of Your maidservant and remember me,
and not forget Your maidservant,
but will give Your maidservant a son,
then I will give him to the Lord all the days of his life,
and a razor shall never come on his head"
(1 Samuel 1:10–11 NASU).

When we women read about women in the Bible, we sit up and take notice. We ask ourselves, "Can we identify with her?" or "Have we ever met someone like her?" In most instances, we can answer yes.

We can identify with Hannah. She wanted a baby—in fact, she begged for a baby. Her heart yearned to rock a baby and raise a baby and love a baby. Those feelings are innate—God given.

Hannah's husband was a good man, and he loved Hannah very much. But Elkanah had a very big problem—two wives. Have you ever read of a peaceful home with one man and more than one wife? God permitted the Israelites to have multiple wives, but His original design was one woman for one man. There were surely too many cooks in Elkanah's kitchen.

## A JEALOUS RIVAL

Peninnah, the other wife, constantly taunted Hannah and mocked her inability to bear children. Listen to how God describes Peninnah:

> And her rival also provoked her severely, to make her miserable, because the Lord had closed her womb. So it was, year by year, when she went up to the house of the Lord, that [Peninnah] provoked her; therefore she wept and did not eat (1 Samuel 1:6–7 NKJV).

Peninnah and Elkanah had children together, but Peninnah seemed to know that Elkanah loved Hannah very much. Perhaps Peninnah had heard Elkanah ask Hannah: "Am I not better to you than ten sons?" (1 Samuel 1:8). So Peninnah delighted to point out Hannah's shortcomings and the most important thing that separated them—motherhood. Israelite women considered their children a mark of personal worth. Being barren was a fate worse than death.

> Be sure when making judgements to have all evidence . . . don't be quick to jump to conclusions.

God closed Hannah's womb. Why? We can only speculate, but don't you suppose God's timing played a major part in Hannah's becoming a mother? He was waiting for Hannah to prepare herself for a special child. But Hannah considered her plight as an "affliction" (1 Samuel 1:11), a curse—a dreaded disease for women only.

The scenario of jealousy between Hannah and Peninnah probably repeated itself many times through the years: "It happened year after year . . . she would provoke her" (1 Samuel 1:7). Oh, how Peninnah loved to get her barbs in. Each year Hannah went up to the house of the Lord and returned home the same way. Except this year—this year would be different.

## A VOW AT THE BEGGING PLACE

This year in Shiloh, Hannah ate, drank, and rose to go to the temple. In great distress, she cried and prayed to God. "Greatly distressed" means "bitter of soul." How appropriate. Hannah's soul was bitter—tormented—because her arms were still empty.

## HANNAH'S VOW

"And she made a vow" (1 Samuel 1:11). Have you ever been vexed in spirit? Have you ever pleaded with the Lord and made heart-felt promises when you were absolutely desperate? Most of my sisters in Christ understand these desperate prayers! Well, Hannah prayed desperately—only this time she made a vow. And making a vow is serious business—then and now. A vow is a "solemn promise by which one binds himself." Hannah made a solemn promise; she fully intended to keep it.

Here is how God feels about vows: "When you make a vow to God, do not delay to pay it; for He has no pleasure in fools. Pay what you have vowed—better not to vow than to vow and not pay" (Ecclesiastes 5:4–5 NKJV). God is saying, "When you make a vow to Me, you had better keep it. A promise is a promise." Actually, we lie when we do not honor a vow, and who would dare lie to God? (We have a saying around our house: "If you lie, you fry!")

What did Hannah vow? She vowed that if God would give her a son, she would give him back to the Lord all the days of his life and that his hair would never be cut. The part of her vow about the hair is a Nazirite vow (Numbers 6). The Nazirite vow was usually just for a period of time, but Hannah vowed never to let the child's hair be cut. She felt so strongly about having a son that she took the Nazirite vow a step further. Oh, how she wanted a child!

## FALSELY ACCUSED!

What was Eli, the priest, thinking as he watched Hannah in prayer, her lips moving silently? He thought she was drunk. Drunken worshipers might have been common in those days of moral decay in Israel. Eli's own sons stole sacrificial food and committed adultery with the women who came to worship. How absolutely disgusting! But Hannah was far from being drunk. She was praying as fervently and earnestly as she could. Of all things to be accused of—and in the house of the Lord on top of that!

What is the lesson for us? We must be sure, when making judgments, to have all available evidence before us. The admonition is clear for us today: don't be quick to jump to conclusions.

When Hannah learned what Eli was thinking, she replied calmly, "No, my lord, I am a woman of sorrowful spirit. I have drunk neither wine nor intoxicating drink, but have poured out my soul before the

Lord" (1 Samuel 1:15 NKJV). Hannah was not busy pouring out wine for herself but busy pouring out her soul to God. Pouring out one's soul is more than a promise. It is spilling one's heart, one's soul, one's desire as fervently as possible at the throne of the Father. It is a vow. The Begging Place is a place of vows.

## GOD ANSWERED HANNAH'S PRAYER!

God said yes! Do we ever consider how much our Father loves to say yes? He loves His children like we love ours—even more. One of my favorite Scriptures is 1 John 3:1: "Behold what manner of love the Father has bestowed on us, that we should be called children of God!" (NKJV). God wants to give us the desires of our hearts because He is our Father. And fathers want their children to be happy. Our Father does say yes.

### LORD, YOU LOVE TO SAY YES

Lord, I asked You for abundant life,
Rich, challenging, full of adventure,
And You said Yes.
I asked You for an undisturbable joy,
Independent of transitory change,
And You said Yes.
I asked You to thread my tears into a song,
When I was shattered and torn with grief,
And You said Yes.
I asked You to steady me when I staggered—
To hold me when I struggled,
To seize me when I resisted,
And You said Yes.
I asked You to forgive my vain grasping,
My foolish fears, my willful pride,
And You said Yes.
I asked You to be my Helper, my Friend,
My Light in the darkness,
And You said Yes.
I asked You to guide me all my life
With Your wisdom, Your counsel,
Your captivating love,
And You said Yes.

Sometimes, Lord,
I feel like a spoiled child
Who gets whatever he asks for.
You overwhelm me with joy,
For You love to say Yes!

—Ruth Harms Calkin

If God loved Hannah, why was she childless? Because God had a bigger plan in mind, and God was moving forward with His plan. So Hannah poured out her soul before the Lord and made a soul-binding vow. God knew how powerful and useful Samuel would be, but first Elkanah and Hannah had to realize their awesome responsibilities in training him for God. In other words, God first had to prepare Hannah and Elkanah.

Hannah's vow was incredible, and her commitment to that vow was as true and real and honest as the woman she was. Hannah was no ordinary woman, and her son was to be no ordinary prophet.

## GOD REMEMBERED

Eli's parting words to Hannah were words of comfort, and her trip home was probably shorter than before. I often wonder if Peninnah saw a change in her. If she didn't right away, she would soon enough, because of those marvelous words in 1 Samuel 1:19: "the Lord remembered her."

Our Father hears and answers our prayers. He sometimes grants our requests, but many times He says, "No, that's not good for you." We don't always understand, but learning to lean on our Lord and learning to trust in Him result from building a good prayer life. Learning to make everything right and keep everything right is essential for maintaining a clear conscience. That is the relationship I want with my Father.

Imagine the Lord saying to you,

God had a bigger plan in mind, and God was moving forward with His plan.

For I know the thoughts [or plans] that I think toward you . . . thoughts of peace and not of evil, to give you a future and a hope. Then you will call upon Me and go and pray to Me, and I will listen to you. And you will seek Me and find Me, when you search for Me with all your heart (Jeremiah 29:11–13 NKJV).

You see, with the Lord it is all or nothing at all. And that is what Hannah learned that day in Shiloh.

### ANY REGRETS?

Imagine Hannah's trip home. Did she replay every word over and over in her mind? She had pleaded her case before the Lord; Eli had spoken words of hope, and now she waited. She must not have waited very long, because in due time she gave birth to a son. How Hannah's heart must have sung and rejoiced during her pregnancy! She no longer felt the affliction of barrenness; she was finally fulfilled. Suddenly her jealous rival had no words of torment—just silence. We don't read anything else about that mean Peninnah. Our vengeful natures are thrilled that she finally got her just reward. But don't forget, Hannah had made a vow to give her son back to the Lord. Hannah's greatest test was still before her.

> Instead of collapsing or crying or wailing, she prayed and sang a mighty song of thanksgiving.

Hannah evidently knew how long she would keep Samuel at home and how she would prepare him for his next home. All of us know of a mother's love for her child. Perhaps there were times when Hannah wanted to cancel her vow. But to have gone back on her word would have been unthinkable. Hannah remembered her vow was unlike any other. It was made in the very presence of God. Can't you hear her saying over and over: "A promise is a promise"? There was no turning back.

Hannah was a remarkable woman. We know what it is like to guide our own child by the hand and then hand him over to someone else and walk away. There is usually great screaming, crying, and carrying on by both mother and child. Hannah must have prepared herself and Samuel for their parting. I imagine that every day as she rocked and talked to her son, she told him the day was coming when they both would travel to his new home with Eli in Shiloh.

Think of the things she might have told Samuel. She must have described Eli, the tabernacle, and some of his duties there. She taught him to love the Lord and to want to please Him. She knew how hard the parting would be for both of them, and she realized how foolish she would be if she caused Samuel to fall apart. I think she was in control of this parting, and she must have made sure that it went as smoothly as possible.

## HANNAH'S SONG

Hannah reminded Eli who she was when she presented Samuel to him. She repeated her promise of dedicating Samuel to the Lord:

> O my lord! As your soul lives, my lord, I am the woman who stood by you here, praying to the Lord. For this child I prayed, and the Lord has granted me my petition which I asked of Him. Therefore I also have lent him to the Lord; as long as he lives he shall be lent to the Lord (1 Samuel 1:26–28 NKJV).

Instead of collapsing or crying or wailing, she prayed and sang a mighty song of thanksgiving. She didn't sing a song of how wonderful her little boy was, or how much she would miss him. Instead, she praised God and His omnipotence, His omnipresence, and His omniscience. How similar her song was to another remarkable woman's song from the New Testament. In Luke 1:46–55 we find the marvelous song of Mary, the mother of Jesus, who sang of God's magnificence. Mary's song and Hannah's song are much alike in praising God, His holiness, and His strength. Over and over in these songs we see the deliverance of the lowly and the elevation of the poor and barren. What marvelous songs these women sang—all to the glory of God!

## SPEAK LORD, I AM LISTENING

What happened to Hannah? I am so grateful to our sweet Father for these words: "And the Lord visited Hannah, so that she conceived and bore three sons and two daughters" (1 Samuel 2:21 NKJV). Thank You, God, for blessing Hannah again and again. Thank You for delivering her from her vengeful rival, Peninnah.

I admire Hannah. She is a portrait of what God wants women to be. And she is a portrait of what God expects mothers to be. Hannah was honest, true, and dependable. She could be counted on to do what she promised. She knew that God had all the answers and that He would hear her earnest prayer for a son. She dedicated her son to the Father mentally, even before she physically rocked him. The lesson is clear: Women must make plans for their children to be raised in the Lord, even before they are born. This is no last-minute decision. Had Hannah not kept her promise, her son Samuel might never have become the mighty prophet God had in mind. What is the value of a mother's vow and dedication to the Lord? It is priceless.

> Samuel was dedicated to the Lord. Oh, that we would dedicate our children to God, and plan and encourage them to total commitment to Him. How many of us would rejoice if our children should leave us to take the gospel to the whole world? Too few, I am afraid. "Stay with me," is our cry, too often. "Don't take my grandkids away" (Lea Fowler, *Precious in the Sight of God* [Quality Publications: Abilene, TX, 1983], 47–48).

God heard and answered Hannah's begging prayer. He knew her heart just as He knows ours as we come to meet Him at the Begging Place. He was not disappointed in Hannah. She kept her vow. What about us? Do we keep our promises to God? Have we trained our children to serve the Lord? Do our children say, "Speak, Lord, I am listening"? It is a sobering thought, isn't it?

## THOUGHTS TO PONDER

1. What was Elkanah's biggest problem?

2. How did Eli help Hannah?

3. What important promise to God did Hannah keep?

4. List other blessings Hannah received from God.

## SONG FOR TODAY

### SAVIOR, GRANT ME REST AND PEACE

Savior, grant me rest and peace,
Let my troubled dreamings cease;
With the chiming midnight bell,
Teach my heart that "all is well."

I would trust my all with Thee,
All my cares and sorrows flee,
Till the breaking light shall tell
Night is past, and "all is well."

I would seek Thy service, Lord,
Leaning on Thy promise-word;
Let my hourly labors tell
I am Thine, and "all is well."

## PRAYER FOR TODAY

*Our dear Lord, we thank You so much for hearing our every prayer. As Your children, we are so grateful that You understand what we are trying to express to You even when we cannot find the right words. We are humbled as we journey through this life and feel Your constant presence. Thank You, O God, for the endearing story of Hannah, who desperately wanted children of her own. Our hearts go out to her. We women understand her feelings, her prayers, her desperation, and her vow to You. Please help us to learn to be patient and long-suffering, like You are with us. Your will be done, and not ours. Thank You for loving us. In Jesus' name. Amen.*

# BECKY'S MEMORIES

## THE DISTRESS CURE—SURRENDER

Our son-in-law was sent to Iraq two years ago. I have never prayed so hard for anything as I prayed for his safety. I asked our home congregation to pray for him. I asked the sisters at ladies' days where I was speaking to please pray for our Tim. I often fasted as I prayed for him. I chose several times a day to get on my knees to pray for him. I went to the Begging Place over and over and over—many times with tears. I imagined myself walking into God's throne room, prostrating myself at His feet, and beseeching Him over and over to deliver Tim. I remembered that Jesus was interceding for me and reminding God how much mothers love their children. I was comforted that the Holy Spirit made my prayers pleasing to God.

Our daughter once told me that Tim's favorite hymn was "When Peace Like a River." When we sang this song in church, I choked up. I could not sing. Tears welled up in my eyes and I prayed that Tim would again be singing this with us one day. God heard my prayer, and the prayers of others, too. Our Tim came back to us safe and sound. I simply cannot describe the joy and thankfulness in my heart. Many times since then we have sung "When Peace Like a River" in worship. Tim sings it with gusto. I look at my daughter, and we smile into each other's eyes, knowing what the other is thinking—and I still cannot sing this song.

Let's listen to a Christian mother with a son in the military and see what she has to say about prayer:

> I go to sleep praying, and I wake up praying. My son, Lt. Col. Bob Bishop, along with his reserve unit, was put on alert as preparations for the invasion of Iraq were beginning. In February he and his unit were deployed to Kuwait. He has believed all his life that he is here on earth to help make the world a better place, and he has never hesitated when he was called to active duty.
>
> We have been a military family. Bob's father served in the military at the end of World War II and in Korea. All my married life I have depended on a higher power for strength and comfort. I have learned that God is able to do far more than I can understand . . . God has always been there for me. My husband had his first heart attack while stationed in Germany. He was only 42; he died a few years later with another heart attack. I had two teenage sons and

so I had to depend even more on God. Without prayer and Jesus I would have nothing to depend on.

I have learned that prayer is more than praise of God or asking God for our needs. Prayer is surrendering my will to God's will. What I am asking for becomes less significant to me than knowing what God is asking of me. Surrender is what prayer brings to my life. (Aileen Bishop, a retired elementary school teacher, is a member of the Sixth and Izard church, Little Rock, Arkansas. Article is from *Christian Chronicle*, 2004.)

## CHAPTER 6

# FIRST PRAYERS

*And these words, which I am commanding*

*you today, shall be on your heart . . .*

*teach them diligently to your sons . . .*

*talk of them when you sit in your house*

*and when you walk by the way*

*and when you lie down and when you rise up . . .*

*bind them as a sign on your hand and*

*they shall be as frontals on your forehead . . .*

*write them on the doorposts*

*of your house and on your gates*

*(Deuteronomy 6:6-9).*

Now I lay me down to sleep,
I pray the Lord my soul to keep.
If I should die before I wake,
I pray the Lord my soul to take.

I remember my first prayer. I did not know what all the words meant, but I did know bedtime was the time to stop and ask our Father in heaven to watch over us as we slept.

Bill Cosby said that, as a boy, when he got to the "if I should die" part, that did it—he wasn't going to sleep at all. On a more serious note, a woman recently diagnosed with stage-four cancer—already being dosed with morphine daily—confessed that this child's verse was her favorite prayer. She sobbed through her tears, "'If I should die before I wake' is too real for me."

What was your first prayer? You can probably say it to yourself right now. Who taught you that prayer? Most likely it was your mother or father. Perhaps it was a grandmother. Regardless of who was looking after you, most likely you were introduced to prayer at an early age.

## As a Child

As a college student, I was struggling with my prayer life. I confessed to Mother my hesitancy in saying prayers out loud at dorm devos. She looked at me and said, "Becky, when you say a prayer, you are just talking to the Lord. You are telling Him what is on your mind and in your heart. That's all." That helped me, not only to become more intimate with God, but also to overcome the fear of saying a prayer out loud.

How about praying at mealtime? We have all heard: "God is great. God is good. Let us thank Him for our food." My husband's grandfather was notorious for saying, "Thank you for this food. Pass the biscuits, please." Short and to the point.

Have you ever listened to a child say the blessing for the food? A child will mention every single dish on the table—all the vegetables, salt and pepper—and the dog, as well. Our son Jeffrey was a prime example of this. His typical prayer was, "Dear God, thank You for our food, our potatoes, our fried chicken, our corn, our salad, our rolls, our tea, and whatever that brown stuff is over there in the flowered dish. In Jesus' name, Amen."

> Children do not have any problem with praying and talking to God.

A sweet sister from Nashville told me of her grandson's prayer. He was praying for God to watch over his parents. Then he started naming his grandparents and great grandparents. He was asking God to help his great grandmother get well, when he suddenly remembered that she had passed on. So he said, "Oh, well, tell Grandmother hello for me." Surely God smiled at his efforts.

Look at the following incident during Jesus' ministry:

At that time the disciples came to Jesus, saying, "Who then is greatest in the kingdom of heaven?" And He called a child to Himself and set him before them, and said, "Truly I say to you, unless you are converted and become like children, you shall not enter the kingdom of heaven. Whoever then humbles himself as this child, he is the greatest in the kingdom of heaven" (Matthew 18:1–4).

What was Jesus expressing to those who want to do His will? The answer is easy. If we want to enter the kingdom of heaven, we must change—be converted—and become like children, who by nature are humble, honest, trusting, accepting, and loving. Children do not have any problem with praying and talking to God.

What happens if we don't change and become childlike? Look at verse 3 again: "Truly I say to you, Unless you are converted and become like children, you shall not enter the kingdom of heaven."

Brother Marshall Keeble commented on this passage:

> Jesus said, "Except ye become as little children, you can't enter the kingdom of God." The trouble with those of us in the church is that everybody wants to be grown up. We don't have a child-like disposition. Everybody wants to be big, so they end up going around splitting churches (Cato, *His Hand and Heart*, 51).

Children are pleasing to God because they have the best attitude. They are by nature sweet, gut honest, and anxious to please—most of the time. They say exactly what they are feeling. They believe whatever they are told is the truth. Children will apologize quickly to make peace—and to avoid punishment. (They are very smart, too.) And when a child prays, he prays sincerely and from his heart. To him, God is very real and very present. It is no wonder that God loves children the way He does. And it is no wonder that we should be like them.

## WHOSE JOB IS IT?

Parents need to consider the importance of praying with their children and listening to them pray. How interesting that prayer and singing are the first spiritual things we learn to do as children. Prayer is a most important first step. In praying to God, we learn there is a God and that He listens to everything we say. This is the beginning of our faith.

## LORD, ARE YOU SERIOUS?

Lord, do I really have to do everything You say?
Don't I get to do some things my very own way?
Isn't your book just full of suggested things to do?
Hints full of wisdom, proposals, often true?
Or are Your words still "wonderful words of life"?
Could they really have the power to quench my pride and strife?
Surely in all this time they've lost some of their power,
Can no longer give the strength to each waking hour.
But a solemn thought keeps probing as it ever comes my way.
The words I've said will judge me when we meet on Judgment Day!

—Lea Fowler

We sometimes become so busy making a living and solving problems that we forget the importance of talking to our children about the Lord. Too many Christians feel it is the church's responsibility to raise their children and get them to heaven. Nothing is further from the truth! How can the church in four hours a week instill all the knowledge, all the lessons, all the wisdom, and all the warnings every child should know? It is impossible. (And the four hours a week applies only to those who are faithful in attendance!)

When we consider this, perhaps we realize why God made families in the first place. It was God's intention for mothers and fathers to faithfully and diligently instruct their children to please Him, to know Him, and to obey His Word. If mothers and fathers desire faithful and obedient children who will obey God, then they must be faithful and obedient themselves. If going to heaven is our goal, then we will talk about heaven continually. This is God's formula for faithful and happy families—talking about spiritual things, talking about Him. Discussing the creation at the supper table. Playing "the guessing game" with Bible characters while riding in the car. When the entire family is pleasing to God and seeking to learn more about Him, life is good. The blessings that God will pour down from heaven will be sweet, bountiful, and unbelievable!

> How can the church in four hours a week instill all the knowledge . . . all the wisdom, and all the warnings every child should know?

God never leaves us in the dark about what to teach our children. His curriculum is woven all through His Word. Consider these passages:

> Hear, O Israel! The Lord is our God, the Lord is one! And you shall love the Lord your God with all your heart and with all your soul and with all your might. And these words, which I am commanding you today, shall be on your heart; and you shall teach them diligently to your sons and shall talk of them when you sit in your house and when you walk by the way and when you lie down and when you rise up. And you shall bind them as a sign on your hand and they shall be as frontals on your forehead. And you shall write them on the doorposts of your house and on your gates (Deuteronomy 6:4–9).

> And all your sons will be taught of the Lord; and the well-being of your sons will be great (Isaiah 54:13).

> "Let not a wise man boast of his wisdom, and let not the mighty man boast of his might, let not a rich man boast of his riches; but let him who boasts, boast of this, that he understands and knows Me, that I am the Lord who exercises lovingkindness, justice, and righteousness on earth; for I delight in these things," declares the Lord (Jeremiah 9:23–24).

> Now therefore, O sons, listen to me, for blessed are they who keep my ways. Heed instruction and be wise, and do not neglect it. Blessed is the man who listens to me, watching daily at my gates, waiting at my doorposts. For he who finds me finds life, and obtains favor from the Lord. But he who sins against me injures himself; all those who hate me love death (Proverbs 8:32–36).

## MOTHERS, WAKE UP!

God's little "How To" book is found in Deuteronomy 6:4–9. In it He instructs His children how to raise faithful and dedicated children, obedient both to their parents and to God.

Isn't obedience natural? Absolutely not. The Bible teaches that we are by nature children of wrath (Ephesians 2:3). Reflect on your own childhood. Did you innately know the right thing to do? No, all of us had to be taught. (If you were stubborn as I was, it probably took you quite some time before you yielded to the final answer.) The same applies to our children today. If we want obedient children, then we have to use every possible opportunity to teach godly lessons and principles. Children have to be taught over and over again. They have to hear the commands of God; they have to listen to them as they go about their daily routines. Teaching goes on when you walk, when you lie down, when you are riding, and when you are sitting. Someone has to talk and talk and talk. And that someone is not the Sunday school teacher or the preacher. That someone is a parent.

Since mothers usually spend more time with their children than fathers do, the woman has a great teaching responsibility. She is the master artist, forming and molding her precious children's lives and souls. Her name is not Monet or Picasso or Van Gogh; she is Mama. And her impact reaches across the face of this earth. Abraham Lincoln said, "All that I am, or hope to be, I owe to my angel mother." Another sage has said, "The hand that rocks the cradle is the hand that rules the world."

Did you ever stop to consider why God made women more verbal than men? He knew who would be spending the most time with the children. Women are quick and skillful at nurturing, caring, teaching, and honing in on what is important for their children. We are naturals at seeing needs and identifying broken hearts and hurting homes. We are spiritual creatures that are sensitive to God and to His will for our families.

## THAT IT MAY BE WELL WITH YOU

The adage "history repeats itself" is true. How many of you have heard your mother's words come out of your own mouth—words that you promised yourself you would never say? (Talk about eating your own words!) We all have experienced that. It must be human nature. But the great thing about history repeating itself is that if you were raised in a strong Christian home, you most likely are raising your children in that same atmosphere. You, too, are talking to your children constantly and instructing them in the nurture and the admonition of the Lord.

Look at how the psalmist said it: "One generation shall praise Thy works to another, and shall declare Thy mighty acts" (Psalm 145:4). Whose works will be praised and whose mighty acts shall be told? Our Lord God's works. Who will do the praising and the declaring? The parents. If the saying is true, "the church is just one generation away from apostasy," then don't let it be our generation that stops teaching our children. Let it not be us who defy God. How absolutely despicable is the idea that in our generation, the church apostatizes. What Christian wants to stand before God Almighty on Judgment

Day and confess, "It was I, Lord. I did not think it was important to teach my children Your ways and Your laws and Your book"?

Notice God's wonderful promises to His children: "O Israel, you should listen and be careful to do it, that it may be well with you and that you may multiply greatly" (Deuteronomy 6:3).

What does "that it may be well with you" mean? That one's life will be good and pleasant. "That you may multiply" describes God's blessings of material things. We must teach our children God's laws, and our lives will be blessed by Him. But do not neglect the admonition in the first part of the verse: "You should listen and be careful to do it."

*. . . the Master Artist . . . Her name is not Monet or Picasso or Van Gogh; she is Mama.*

Look at the two-fold promise written by Paul:

> Children, obey your parents in the Lord, for this is right. Honor your father and mother (which is the first commandment with a promise), that it may be well with you, and that you may live long on the earth (Ephesians 6:1–3; cf. Exodus 20:12).

So God made two promises to those who obey their parents: a good life and a long life. Honoring one's parents has been God's plan from the beginning.

## WHO'S THE BOSS?

When I speak to a group of young mothers, I always elaborate on the importance of Scriptures that tell us how to raise children. Our children are from our bodies. We would fight for them—die for them!—no questions asked. A mother bear's ferocious spirit has nothing on us. A female grizzly with cubs or a human mother whose child is in danger is a powerful force!

How important is it to teach our children to respect our authority? God has given us these precious little ones to raise; we must take that seriously. If we do not teach our children to respect our authority, how will they learn to respect God's authority? If our children will not obey us, they certainly will not obey the Lord.

If you are a new parent or a young parent, may I say something just to you? You must win! Don't let your children run your home. My mother used to say, "Don't let the inmates run the asylum!"

Your house will be in complete chaos if the children are in charge. God assigned those precious children to you. Do not abdicate your responsibility. They will try their best to wear you down so you will surrender to their desires. Someone has to be the "boss," and it should be the parent. How utterly disgusting is a home where children rule!

Remember the television program *Nanny-911?* It is about a home completely out of control because spoiled children are running it.

> "Everything in the modern home is run with a switch, except the child."

The parents, tired and exhausted, try to cope with children who have the audacity to hit, kick, and spit on their parents while shouting obscenities. These wonderful little creatures also never go to bed. They throw fits and rarely eat what Mom has prepared. The parents engage an English nanny, who sets the house back in order and saves the day. The unruly and foul-mouthed children are disciplined by being placed in time-out corners. Never are they spanked. Dr. Phil would agree, I am sure. But what does God say?

- ✠ "He who spares his rod hates his son, but he who loves him disciplines him diligently" (Proverbs 13:24).

- ✠ "Discipline your son while there is hope, and do not desire his death" (Proverbs 19:18).

- ✠ "Foolishness is bound up in the heart of a child; the rod of discipline will remove it far from him" (Proverbs 22:15). (My Mother loved this one!)

- ✠ "Do not hold back discipline from the child, although you beat him with the rod, he will not die. You shall beat him with the rod, and deliver his soul from Sheol" (Proverbs 23:13–14).

- ✠ "The rod and reproof give wisdom, but a child who gets his own way brings shame to his mother" (Proverbs 29:15).

- ✠ "Correct your son, and he will give you comfort; he will also delight your soul" (Proverbs 29:17).

Under Moses' law, a disobedient son was taken outside the city and stoned (Deuteronomy 21:18–21). How grateful I am that we are no longer under that covenant but under the New Testament! Otherwise, many families would be minus a few children!

"Experts" in child rearing do not advocate spanking. Their belief is contrary to God's law. Naturally we must administer discipline under the proper guidelines—always teaching with love, never abusing the child. Abuse is never endorsed by God. There are times for the time-out chair, and then there are some times for "posterior administration" with your favorite switch or other appropriate devise. When I watch *Nanny-911*, I come to the same conclusion: both the nanny and the parents need to be spanked!

## Teach Respect: Be a Light

God gave us the concept of the family. When children love their parents, respect parental authority, and obey the rules of the home, then that home will be what God wants it to be. When children are trained to love God, respect His authority, and obey His laws, then there is no problem with their yielding to the authority of God and His Son's church when they are older. This training is the best gift Christian parents can give their children! You, dear parent, are showing your children how to "walk the walk"!

Parents who talk openly about God and obey His will set the most important example they possibly can. But don't forget this one important factor: parents are the light that guides children to the Lord. Our children are watching us at all times. What examples do they see? What laws do we follow, God's or man's? And are we in subjection to the authority of God?

Willie Cato records brother Keeble's words about the home:

- "If you want purity in your own house, have it first in your own life."
- "Everything in the modern home is run with a switch, except the child. But there can be no improvement on God's plan: 'No chastening for the present seemeth to be joyous, but grievous: nevertheless afterward it yieldeth the peaceable fruit of righteousness unto them which are exercised thereby' " (Hebrews 12:11 KJV). No! Nobody enjoys it, but it has to be done."

- "The one who has the keys runs the home. If you want to ruin your boy or girl, just give them the key and let them come and go when they want to, then you don't run the home—the one who has the key runs it" (Cato, *His Hand and Heart*, 112–113).

## When They See Us Pray

If parents talk about God, their children will talk about God. If parents pray to God, their children will pray to God. But more important, parents praying with their children establishes a pattern. Children mimic their parents. When they hear us rejoice about an answered prayer, they will learn how God works in their lives.

> If a child leaves the Lord in spite of having grown up in a genuine Christian home, that is his choice.

However, if children hear us criticize the preacher on the way home from worship, they learn to be critical of spiritual things. If we are not faithful in worship, our children are not likely to be faithful. How many times have I heard heartbroken Christian parents who have not set the right example wail and cry because their children are involved in illicit lifestyles? "Where did we go wrong?" they cry. Oh, how I wanted to say, "Let me count the ways."

On the other hand, there are wonderful Christians whose children have brought them great despair and anguish. Those situations, too, are heartbreaking.

## What Does It Take to Get Them to Heaven?

Parents must always be aware of their influence on their children. Be careful. Souls are at stake. Our goal for our children should not be a perfect score on the SATs or the best Ivy League college money can buy or a lifestyle with the "best" of everything. Our goal is to get them to heaven. That does not just happen. Know where they are at all times. Have their friends over so you can see who else is influencing them. Love them enough to say no—and stick to it. Listen to them when they try to express themselves. Make sure they prepare their Bible lessons before Sunday morning and Wednesday evening. Teach them about modesty and virginity. Properly influencing our children takes work, communication, involvement, example, understanding, discipline, and a whole lot of love and prayer. Asking God daily for wisdom in raising children is the smartest move any parent can make. I know God and His wisdom have raised my children—not I.

If a child leaves the Lord in spite of having grown up in a genuine Christian home, that is his choice. The following anonymous article illustrates the power of choice.

## BLAMING GODLY PARENTS
## FOR UNGODLY BEHAVIOR

A young person decides to quit the church and launch out into the world of sin and shame. When approached by some interested person he says, "I have had religion rammed down my throat all my life." Thus, his brokenhearted parents are made to take the blame for his sin. How inhuman and cruel can one be?

I had food "rammed down my throat" all my life, and I still love to eat. I was made to comb my hair and take a bath all my life, but I still comb my hair and bathe. My mother tried in an uneducated sort of way to teach me right from wrong, and though I have done many things wrong, it never occurred to me to blame my mother for any misbehavior on my part.

My wife and I never rammed religion down our children's throats, unless that is what you call trying to bring them up "in the nurture and admonition of the Lord." I can name five young people who have thus accused their parents. These young people ought to go to their parents, get on their knees before them, and beg for their forgiveness for such base ingratitude, and go with them before God and ask His forgiveness.

Young people, if you must be ungodly, don't blame godly parents. All they ever wanted for you was that you live right. Be a man or a woman, and face your mistakes. You will give an account at the Judgment.

The wonderful proverb, "Train up a child in the way he should go, even when he is old he will not depart from it" (Proverbs 22:6), is not an absolute. Our kids can and will make foolish mistakes and poor choices. What can we do? Pray. Pray for the child and pray for time.

## THOUGHTS TO PONDER

1. Why is it important to pray with your child?

2. How is humility exhibited in children?

3. What is God's formula in Deuteronomy 6:4–9 for raising children?

4. What is the double promise in Ephesians 6:1–3?

## SONG FOR TODAY

### DEAR LORD AND FATHER OF MANKIND

Dear Lord and Father of mankind,
Forgive our foolish ways.
Reclothe us in our rightful mind,
In purer lives Thy service find,
In deeper rev'rence praise.

In simple trust like theirs who heard,
Beside the Syrian sea,
The gracious calling of the Lord,
Let us, like them, without a word,
Rise up and follow Thee.

Drop thy still dews of quietness,
Till all our strivings cease.
Take from our souls the strain and stress,
And let our ordered lives confess
The beauty of Thy peace. Amen.

## PRAYER FOR TODAY

*Dear God in heaven, thank You for this moment in time. Thank You that we are alive and that things are as well with us as they are. Father, we praise You for being our Father and for loving us. How kind You are to give us children and families and to surround us with people to love. We all need love, and we all need Your love most of all. Please forgive us of our sins. Help us to do better tomorrow. In Jesus' name. Amen.*

# BECKY'S MEMORIES

## GO TO YOUR ROOM!

My hat is off to schoolteachers. Other than motherhood, it is the hardest and most stressful job in the world, in my opinion. First, you must know your material. Second, you try to teach that material. Sound easy? It is not. While you are trying to teach, your students are trying to keep you from teaching. A hand is constantly in the air, someone is knocking at the door, a kid is trying to throw up on your desk—and you are attempting to teach *Great Expectations*. You go home, brain dead, of course, and your work begins again. You have papers to grade, parents are calling, and you are mentally planning for the next day. Your family is shortchanged.

My mother was a music teacher. She had this advice for anyone thinking of pursuing the field of education: "You need a whip and a chair—and I taught something that was fun." Man, was she right! Every schoolteacher in this country ought to be paid a hundred thousand dollars a week. (I have not had a teacher disagree with me on that yet!) Those of other professions ask, "What can possibly be so hard about teaching school?" Ask the throngs of teachers who leave each year. Most people do not have a clue as to what it is like to be a schoolteacher. A teacher is like Daniel—all alone in the lions' den!

Now don't get me wrong; there are wonderful kids out there and wonderful teachers, too. Sometimes the teacher has her kids in the palm of her hand, taking them to the sky. And they want to go. Those times are precious, but few and far between.

I once taught an eighth grade class from hell. Honestly, I am not using foul language. They were heathens from the word go! I was absolutely positive that the school bus picked them up at the gates of hell in the morning and dropped them off there at the end of the day. Trust me on this. Were they stupid? Absolutely not. They were brilliant. But they chose to make everyone as miserable as they were. Unruly; no manners; perverse in nature; extremely clever. And many of them were from Christian families. I begged their parents for help. Nothing happened. The principal could never be found when a teacher needed him. All these factors combined for a disastrous academic Pearl Harbor.

Theirs was the last class period of the day. Everyone was tired by that time, but their mission was to seek and destroy; mine was to teach, challenge, and keep the peace. Our classroom was usually in a state of turmoil, resting "securely" on a powder keg. It was just a matter of time before it blew.

At last someone lit the fuse; they destroyed and conquered me. I got into my car. I cried all the way home. I would have quit, but I did not have the luxury of being independently wealthy. How I dreaded the thought of returning the next day to face those creatures again! Sometimes you hate reality.

I drove home. I drove into my garage. I walked into my home and headed straight for the phone. I called Mom.

"Mom? I can't take it anymore!"

"It's that eighth grade class again, isn't it?" she asked.

"Yes." And I went on to describe the day's explosion.

And, Mom, bless her little heart, came through again. "Becky, here is what you are going to do. Go to your room and get down on your knees. Then imagine a huge, white sheet with four corners. Throw that eighth grade class into it, along with all the problems you are having right now. Then take the four corners and tie them in one big knot. Toss this sheet up as high as you can, and God will catch it. You are giving Him that eighth grade class, and He is going to handle them from now on. They are too much for you. You will get up off your knees. Listen to me, you are not looking back or taking that sheet back! Give it to the Lord and walk away! Now, I am praying for you. Remember, God loves you and you are a child of the King. Now go and do what I say."

I did as my mother told me. I poured out my soul to the Father, and He listened. I finished my prayer, got up off my knees, and walked away. I felt peace for the first time in months.

God caught my sheet. I gave it to Him. I quoted: "Casting all your care upon Him, for He cares for you" (1 Peter 5:7 NKJV).

The New American Standard Version has "anxiety" instead of "care." Peter had cast nets into the sea many times, but he had to pull them back again. But he does not use the fishing term here. This *cast* means to throw something down and walk away, never to pick it up again. Now that is a whole different meaning, isn't it?

God took care of that eighth grade class. The next day I talked with them about their behavior and told them that from then on their behavior was going to be better. I had told them these things before, but this time it was different. They were never wonderful—but they were manageable. For that, I will be grateful to my Father until the day I die. He delivered me from that lions' den.

God has promised He will never leave us nor forsake us. I am glad He is actively involved in the lives of His children. I can go to Him anytime I want and ask for His help. I went to the Begging Place that day, and God heard my supplication. He delivered me from those awful children! Thank You, God. Prayer truly changes things.

And, thank you, Mom.

## CHAPTER 7

# GOOD KING HEZEKIAH

He trusted in the Lord, the God of Israel;
so that after him there was none like him among all
the kings of Judah, nor among those who were before
him. For he clung to the Lord; he did not depart from
following Him, but kept His commandments, which the
Lord had commanded Moses. And the Lord was with
him; wherever he went he prospered
(2 Kings 18:5-7).

What do you know about King Hezekiah? In my Sunday school classes, he was always called "good King Hezekiah." He was one of the few upright and morally good kings in the Old Testament. Events of his life are in 2 Chronicles 29–32; 2 Kings 18–20; and Isaiah 36–39.

Let's examine Hezekiah's background. His father Ahaz was king before him. Explore Ahaz's wickedness in 2 Chronicles 28. He was an idolater, even sacrificing his own children to Baal. He took treasures from the temple of God and gave them to the king of Assyria. These are but a few of Ahaz's atrocities.

## "HE DID RIGHT"

Out of this horror and mayhem, Hezekiah was crowned king of Judah. He reigned twenty-nine years. Hezekiah and Josiah were the only kings of Judah who were as faithful as King David had been. The Bible says, "And he did right in the sight of the Lord, according to all that his father David had done" (2 Chronicles 29:2).

Like the Phoenix rising from the ashes, Hezekiah ascended the throne and completely eradicated all the idolatry his father had established. He destroyed the high places of idolatrous worship. He also destroyed the bronze serpent Moses had made in the wilderness; it had become an object of worship. Perhaps his greatest accomplishment was that of reopening of the temple: "In the first year of his reign, in the first month, he opened the doors of the house of the Lord and repaired them" (2 Chronicles 29:3).

Please note: The opening of the temple occurred the very first month of the first year of Hezekiah's reign. Hezekiah focused on proper worship. He regrouped the Levites and built up the Lord's priesthood. Thousands of animals were sacrificed; the temple was cleansed and rededicated, and the people rejoiced with songs and worshiped God.

> Intelligent people who feast daily at the "trough of what's happening" walk away spiritually anorexic.

Hezekiah was everything his father was not. Ahaz "walked in the ways of the kings of Israel," but Hezekiah "did right in the sight of the Lord." Hezekiah had a good and pleasing heart for God: "Now it is in my heart to make a covenant with the Lord God of Israel, that His burning anger may turn away from us" (2 Chronicles 29:10).

## SPIRITUAL AWAKENING AND UNITY FOR ISRAEL

It always makes me wonder how a man can be so wicked and his son so godly. Surely Hezekiah must have observed the constant idolatrous and evil ways of his father. Why wasn't Hezekiah drawn into idolatry? Did his mother Abijah teach him about the true God? Perhaps his companionship with the prophet Isaiah influenced his love for God. We don't know. We do know that King Hezekiah knew about God and His law. He knew that the previous kings of Judah had led the people into idol worship and that God was angry with His people. How remarkable it is that this king wanted to please God!

Hezekiah initiated a spiritual rebirth in Israel, even though the kingdom had long been divided into two parts. Hezekiah desired to celebrate the Passover again. He sent couriers into the northern kingdom and invited her citizens to come once again to Jerusalem and celebrate the feast that memorialized God's sparing Israel's first-born and the flight of His people from Egypt.

Hezekiah knew animosity existed among the tribes. The tribes of Ephraim, Manasseh, and Zebulun mocked and laughed at the couriers and their invitation to the Passover. However, a few men from

Asher, Manasseh, and Zebulun humbled themselves and came to Jerusalem to celebrate the Passover (2 Chronicles 30:10–11).

How long had it been since Judah and Israel had celebrated the Passover as one people? They had been divided for over two centuries. Hezekiah seemed to have a vision of God's people coming together and celebrating His love and deliverance. He deeply desired unity.

> And thus Hezekiah did throughout all Judah; and he did what was good, right, and true before the Lord his God. And every work which he began in the service of the house of God in law and in commandment, seeking his God, he did with all his heart and prospered (2 Chronicles 31:20–21).

Read more about the relationship between God and Hezekiah:

> He trusted in the Lord, the God of Israel; so that after him there was none like him among all the kings of Judah, nor among those who were before him. For he clung to the Lord; he did not depart from following Him, but kept His commandments, which the Lord had commanded Moses. And the Lord was with him; wherever he went he prospered (2 Kings 18:5–7).

This passage reveals that Hezekiah did three things: he trusted in the Lord, he clung to the Lord, and he did not depart from following the Lord. Why wouldn't God love a person like that? Why then won't more people choose to trust and cling and follow? The answer is the word *choose*.

## TODAY'S SPIRITUAL ANOREXIA

Most do not want to trust, follow, and cling to the Father. That is too simplistic and corny. Gurus, the Dalai Lama, and fashionable psycho-therapists are popular these days. How amazing and absolutely tragic are the numbers of intelligent people who feast daily at the "trough of what's happening" and walk away spiritually anorexic.

Several years ago *Good Morning America* featured one of San Francisco's odd-shaped stone street barriers. A group of San Franciscans decided it was their god. They strung flowers all over it and lit candles at its base. At first glance, I could not help but chuckle, but then I decided theirs was the saddest story in the world. What lengths some people will go to believe anything but the Bible! It takes more faith to worship a stone than it does to believe in God. The big bang theory requires more faith than does Genesis 1:1: "In the beginning God created the heavens and the earth." (I like the bumper sticker that says "I believe in the big bang theory. God said it and *bang*, it was done!")

Today's state of affairs is no surprise to God. Jesus came to the point:

> If any one wishes to come after Me, let him deny himself, and take up his cross, and follow Me. For whoever wishes to save his life shall lose it; but whoever loses his life for My sake shall find it. For what will a man be profited, if he gains the whole world, and forfeits his soul? Or what will a man give in exchange for his soul? (Matthew 16:24–26).

Hezekiah chose to love and serve God, and God blessed him, heard his prayers, and answered those prayers with a positive yes. If the masses knew that choosing to love and serve God makes for a wonderful life—and afterlife—what a difference their faith would make.

## THE FOOLISHNESS OF SENNACHERIB

Good King Hezekiah pleased God, and God blessed him. Even when the nation of Assyria, led by the mighty King Sennacherib, tried to conquer Judah, God delivered the southern kingdom. The Bible is always historically correct, and you will even find that Sennacherib's own diaries mention King Hezekiah. How interesting!

Sennacherib sent messengers in an attempt to undermine Judah's faith in the one true God. His plan backfired. The people of Jerusalem loved their king and witnessed firsthand his trust in God, so they followed Hezekiah's example. Sennacherib was an arrogant heathen. He did not know the power and might of the one true God who loved King Hezekiah.

## HEZEKIAH AND ISAIAH GO TO THE BEGGING PLACE TOGETHER

You've heard it a thousand times: "When the going gets tough, the tough get going." With the Assyrian army surrounding Jerusalem, Hezekiah knew he needed to pray. He went up to the house of the Lord and spread before the Lord a threatening letter from Sennacherib. He prayed:

> O Lord, the God of Israel, who art enthroned above the cherubim, Thou art the God of Israel, Thou alone, of all the kingdoms of the earth, Thou hast made heaven and earth. Incline Thine ear, O Lord, and hear; open Thine eyes, O Lord, and see; and listen to the words of Sennacherib, which he has sent to reproach the living God. Truly, O Lord, the kings of Assyria have devastated the nations and their lands and have cast their gods into the fire, for they were not gods but the work of men's hands, wood and stone. So they have destroyed them. And now, O Lord our God, I pray, deliver us from his hand that all the kingdoms of the earth may know that Thou alone, O Lord, art God (2 Kings 19:15–19).

*"Deliver us . . . that all the kingdoms of the earth may know that Thou alone, O Lord, art God."*

Hezekiah shows great humility when approaching the throne of the Master Creator. His prayer is simple, and so is his request for deliverance. What was God's reaction? "Thus says the Lord, the God of Israel, 'Because you have prayed to Me about Sennacherib king of Assyria, I have heard you'" (2 Kings 19:20).

Why did God hear Hezekiah's prayer? "Because you have prayed to Me." God listened when Hezekiah was at the Begging Place—and He will listen when we are there, too.

## CRYING TO HEAVEN

The account of Hezekiah and Sennacherib has an interesting addition in 2 Chronicles:

> But King Hezekiah and Isaiah the prophet, the son of Amoz, prayed about this and cried out to heaven. And the Lord sent an angel who destroyed every mighty warrior, commander and officer in the camp of the king of Assyria. So he returned in shame to his own land. And when he had entered the temple of his god, some of his own children killed him there with the sword. So the Lord saved Hezekiah and the inhabitants of Jerusalem from the hand of Sennacherib the king of Assyria, and from the hand of all others, and guided them on every side. And many were bringing gifts to the Lord at Jerusalem and choice presents to Hezekiah king

of Judah, so that he was exalted in the sight of all nations thereafter (2 Chronicles 32:20–23).

The Bible states that Hezekiah and Isaiah prayed and cried out to heaven. Both of them sought the Lord, and it seems likely they prayed together. Second Kings 19 says an angel struck the Assyrian camp at night, and 185,000 men were slain. God fought the entire battle for Judah. That is one amazing story. But remember: Hezekiah and Isaiah beseeched the Lord and cried to Him. Crying to heaven involves emotions, tears, and sincere supplications. Their lives, as well as the lives of all the people of Judah, were at stake. The messianic prophet and a good king together went to the Begging Place. The Lord heard their prayers and delivered His people.

Matthew Henry wrote about Isaiah and King Hezekiah and their prayer to God:

> It was a happy time when the king and the prophet joined thus in prayer. Is any troubled? Is any terrified? Let him pray. So we engage God for us; so we encourage ourselves in him. Praying to God is here called *crying to heaven*, because we are, in prayer, to eye him as our Father in heaven, whence he beholds the children of men, and where he has prepared his throne (Henry, *Commentary on the Whole Bible*, 477).

> Lord, give me faith!—to live from day to day,
> With tranquil heart to do my simple part,
> And with my hand in Thine, just go Thy way.
> Lord, give me faith!—to leave it all to Thee,
> The future is Thy gift, I would not lift
> The veil Thy love has hung 'twixt it and me.
>
> —John Oxenham

## HEZEKIAH'S NEAR-DEATH EXPERIENCE

The story of King Hezekiah's illness is what I remember being taught as a young child. Hezekiah was thirty-nine years old when he was struck with a mortal illness. Isaiah brought news to him from God that he was going to die. Hezekiah's heart was broken, and he turned his face to the wall and prayed. "Remember now, O Lord, I pray, how I have walked before You in truth and with a loyal heart, and have done what was good in Your sight" (2 Kings 20:3 NKJV).

Before Isaiah left the court, God instructed him:

> Return and tell Hezekiah the leader of my people, "Thus says the Lord, the God of David your father, 'I have heard your prayer, I have seen your tears; surely I will heal you. On the third day you shall go up to the house of the Lord. And I will add to your days fifteen years. I will deliver you and this city from the hand of the king of Assyria; and I will defend this city for My own sake, and for the sake of My servant David'" (2 Kings 20:5–6 NKJV).

How quickly God answered Hezekiah's prayer to extend his life. Good King Hezekiah was pleading with the Lord with all he had.

## THE SHADOW MIRACLE

Let's also notice Hezekiah's prayer. He reminded God of his loyalty and his accomplishments for Him. Hezekiah was not afraid to be honest with the Lord but was courageous, urging the Lord to recall his walk with Him. With tears, good King Hezekiah fervently presented his case before the Lord, and the Lord not only answered his prayer but also gave him a sign:

> "Behold, I will cause the shadow on the stairway, which has gone down with the sun on the stairway of Ahaz, to go back ten steps." So the sun's shadow went back ten steps on the stairway on which it had gone down (Isaiah 38:8).

God never misses a thing. His actions are always perfect.

> With tears, good King Hezekiah fervently presented his case before the Lord.

## WHAT WAS THE ILLNESS?

Isaiah gives us a clue as to the nature of Hezekiah's illness: "Let them take a cake of figs, and apply it to the boil, that he may recover" (Isaiah 38:21).

Hezekiah's so-called "boil," which was almost fatal, may well have been a true boil or carbuncle. Another suggestion is that is was anthrax. The local application of a poultice of figs has been recognized therapy for gumboils in comparatively recent times. Its use by Hezekiah at the command of God's prophet has often been cited as divine approval of the utilization of medicinal means of therapy (*Pictorial Bible Dictionary* [The Southwestern Company, Zondervan Publishing House: Grand Rapids, MI, 1963], 218).

When Hezekiah became seriously ill, God instructed him to "set thine house in order; for thou shalt die, and not live" (2 Kings 20:1). Hezekiah's fervent prayer, bathed in tears, motivated God to promise him complete recovery within three days. To confirm His promise, God produced a miraculous sign and added fifteen years to his life (Chesser, *Portrait of God*, 163).

## THE LORD WILL SURELY SAVE ME

Good Hezekiah was not a perfect man. He was not a perfect king either. He failed miserably soon after his brush with death. His allies, the Babylonians, came to visit him, and Hezekiah very foolishly showed them his treasuries full of gold, silver, jewels, livestock, and weapons. The Scriptures tell us that there was nothing that he did not show to them. Hezekiah let his pride get in the way of his wisdom.

God permitted Hezekiah a peaceful life. He did not allow the king to see his people carried as slaves to Babylon. God also allowed Hezekiah a peaceful death. God was good to Hezekiah.

## HOPE FROM THE BEGGING PLACE

Was God's decision to extend the king's life a change of mind or was it a test for Hezekiah? The Bible does not reveal the answer. However, this story of God's hearing and answering Hezekiah's prayer so beautifully gives all Christians hope. And hope is one of the main characteristics of the Begging Place. It is always there. The lesson here is simple: God hears the prayers and blesses those who walk with Him and seek His ways. He even turned the hands of time backward for a king whom He loved.

## THOUGHTS TO PONDER

1. Describe King Ahaz, Hezekiah's father.

2. Name several things King Hezekiah did during the first month of his reign.

3. How did Hezekiah feel about God?

4. What did God do for Hezekiah after hearing his prayer for his life in 2 Kings 20?

## SONG FOR TODAY

### SEARCH ME, O GOD

Search me, O God, and know my heart today.
Try me, O Savior, know my thoughts, I pray;
See if there be some wicked way in me;
Cleanse me from every sin, and set me free.

I praise Thee, Lord, for cleansing me from sin,
Fulfill Thy Word, and make me pure within;
Fill me with fire, where once I burned with shame;
Grant my desire to magnify Thy name.

Lord, take my life, and make it wholly Thine,
Fill my poor heart with Thy great love divine;
Take all my will, my passion, self, and pride;
I now surrender, Lord, in me abide.

## PRAYER FOR TODAY

*Dear Father, thank You for giving us this life. May we live it for You and please You with the decisions we make. Father, we ask You for wisdom in all things, especially in our relationships, friendships, and our families. Please forgive our sins and help us to forgive others.*

*We are grateful for the story of Hezekiah and the example that he sets for us in doing the right things, being unafraid to talk to You and pouring his heart out to You. He was surrounded by kings who would not do Your will, but he from the very beginning chose to please You. Thank You for Hezekiah, and thank You, Lord, for answering his prayer and adding more years to his life.*

*Please give us healthy bodies and healthy minds. May we be pleasing in Your sight, too. Please forgive us and help us to seek You every day we live. In Jesus' name. Amen.*

# BECKY'S MEMORIES

## MY HUSBAND'S ARMS

April 2, 2002, began as a beautiful and bright sunny day. I drove to work, praising God and giving Him the glory as I noticed the landscape turning green and beginning to bud with spring. I arrived at the church office and began my usual tasks. My husband called. He simply asked if Scott, our minister, were there. Sensing a problem, I insisted that he tell me what was wrong. Jeff simply said, "Becky, your daddy dropped dead from a heart attack this morning." I could not breathe. All I could do was call Scott to come and help me.

Scott ran into my office and gathered me in his arms. I will never forget what he said: "Well, Becky, your daddy has won the victory." What comfort. I kept repeating those words out loud.

If you have lost a loved one, you know how busy the next several weeks can be after a death. Mom and Dad's home became a beehive of activity with a constant stream of people, food, and phone calls. Both Mom and Dad had written out their wishes. They had chosen their burial plots and headstones. So very little was left to be done. How thankful we all were for their vision and foresight.

Mom did not know who Daddy was, so she was not upset by his death. But she was confused with all the hubbub going on in her house. As we began to take care of her, we quickly realized how much Dad had done for her. She began refusing to swallow. We were completely unsuccessful in getting her to take a bath. Only Daddy could coax her into the shower. We missed Daddy in more ways than one.

At night I put her to bed, sang to her, and kissed her as I tucked her in. She was my little girl now, and I was the mother. She slept for a while, and then started to walk around. I had usually collapsed by the time she got up. Jeff and I set up quarters in Dad's room. Mom would walk into our room and stand by my side of the bed. When I saw her there, I would jump up, tend her needs, guide her back to her room, and tuck her into bed again. An hour later, she would be back by my side of the bed. When morning came, I was exhausted. *How did Daddy do all of this?* I wondered.

Several prayer habits were started that week with Mom. First of all, I started kneeling beside her bed and praying with her at night. Every time I put her to bed, I would kneel and pray that God would bless her, give her peace, and let her sleep. The prayers brought her peace; I returned to my bed.

I often fell into bed crying, grieving my dad's death, frustrated with Mom's nocturnal wanderings and the weighty decisions facing us about her care. My sweet husband would wrap his strong arms around me. hold me, and assure me that things would be fine soon.

One night I just said, "Jeff, pray!" And there in my parent's bed, in the room where Daddy died, Jeff prayed for all of us to have peace and rest. He prayed for God to help Mom in her distress and to help us to make the best decisions about her future. All I could do was hold on to him and weep. All I could manage to say was, "Help us, Father, help us."

This, too, became our prayer habit. Mom continued to appear by the side of the bed; I continued to get up and tend to her. I continued to pray with her and then crawl back into my own bed and cry. Jeff would hold me in his arms as he prayed for God to guide all of us, and we would get about an hour's sleep until it all began again.

Together Jeff and I learned the peace a marriage can have when partners pray together. Surrounded by grief, we traveled to the Begging Place every night and prayed. Sometimes we stayed all night long. We turned to God together, beseeched His will for us and for Mom together, and in the process we became better Christians together. We learned that praying together can strengthen the love partners have for each other. What could be more wonderful than going to the Begging Place, wrapped in the arms of the one you love most on the face of this earth?

There is not a marriage in the world that cannot use God's help. I know that ours certainly could. Who would have thought or imagined that at the time of one's deepest despair, a marriage would experience the peace of heaven? Oh yes, God loves His children.

CHAPTER 8

# DON'T BE A PHARISEE
## (LOOK AT ME! LOOK AT ME!)

And when you pray, you are not to be as the hypocrites;
for they love to stand and pray in the synagogues and
on the street corners, in order to be seen by men.
Truly I say to you, they have their reward in full
(Matthew 6:5).

Have you ever heard a showy prayer? Maybe it was during the worship service—you thought it would never end. Did you check your watch? Did you feel guilty for judging? Come on, be honest. We all have. This phenomenon is nothing new. Men have always prayed just to be seen and heard. Oh, we may not live in that first-century city of Jerusalem, but the Pharisees still pray among us.

There have always been those who pray in a strange manner. You have probably seen orthodox Jews on television praying at the Wailing Wall in Jerusalem. Many of them bobble back and forth as they pray loudly. They truly do wail at the Wailing Wall.

Jesus predicted the fall and total destruction of this temple when He was here on earth. The temple that Solomon built for the Lord had been destroyed by the Babylonians in 586 B.C. With the help of the prophets Haggai, Zachariah, and Malachi, the temple was gradually rebuilt, although it was not the ornate temple that Solomon had built. This temple was desecrated by Antiochus Epiphanes, a Syrian king who forced the high priests to sacrifice swine on the altar in 168 B.C. The Jews and the Maccabees cleansed the temple by replacing the altar stones and rededicated it to God. The Roman consul, Crassus, plundered the gold from the temple in 63 B.C. but did not harm the structure. As far as we know, it was this second structure that Herod the Great revamped and rebuilt. This temple was larger and more beautiful than ever before. It was finally finished by Herod Agrippa in A.D. 64, just six years before Titus completely razed it in A.D. 70 (*Pictorial Bible Dictionary*, 833–834).

Three temples stood successively on Mt. Moriah (2 Chronicles 3:1) in Jerusalem. This site is today called the Haram esh-Sherif and is a Muslim holy place. The first temple was built by Solomon, the second by Zerubbabel and the Jews who returned from the Babylonian exile. The third temple, which was in use in the days of Jesus, was begun and largely built by Herod the Great (*Pictorial Bible Dictionary*, 830).

## NOT AS THE HYPOCRITES

It seems there were showy prayers in Jesus' day, too. In Matthew's account of the *Sermon on the Mount*, Jesus addressed the prayer issue:

> And when you pray, you are not to be as the hypocrites; for they love to stand and pray in the synagogues and on the street corners, in order to be seen by men. Truly I say to you, they have their reward in full. But you, when you pray, go into your inner room, and when you have shut your door, pray to your Father who is in secret, and your Father who sees in secret will repay you. And when you are praying, do not use meaningless repetition, as the Gentiles do, for they suppose that they will be heard for their many words (Matthew 6:5–8).

Jesus called those who prayed to be seen and heard "hypocrites." A hypocrite is someone who pretends to be righteous when he is not. The Greek word *hupokrites* depicts an actor who wears a mask and plays a part. Will God give this kind of person what he has asked for? No.

Jesus instructs us to go into an inner room or a closet and pray. Why? Our prayers are private; they are not for show. I do not believe we have to literally find a closet and pray, but quiet, calm, and peaceful places best serve the Christian's need. It is very difficult to communicate with the Lord while the world passes noisily by.

*Godly men and women in the Bible found places of tranquility for prayers and meditations.*

Matthew Henry makes some very interesting statements about the Matthew 6 passage:

> It is taken for granted that all the disciples of Christ pray. You may as soon find a living man that does not breathe, as a living Christian

that does not pray. If prayerless, then graceless . . . We must not be proud and vain-glorious in prayer, nor aim at the praise of men . . . they prayed in the synagogues, which were indeed proper places for public prayer, but not for personal. They prayed in the corners of the streets, the broad streets which were most frequented. It was to cause themselves to be taken notice of (Henry, *Commentary on the Whole Bible*, 1227).

Let none plead that he does not have a convenient place to privately pray. Isaac retired into the field to pray. The psalmist could be alone with God in the corner of a housetop. If you cannot pray with as much secrecy as you would like, pray anyway. It is doing it with ostentation that is wrong, not doing it under observation when it cannot be avoided (Henry, *Experiencing God's Presence*, 53).

## Quiet Places in the Bible

Godly men and women in the Bible found places of tranquility for prayers and meditations. "And Isaac went out to meditate in the field toward evening; and he lifted up his eyes and looked, and behold, camels were coming" (Genesis 24:63).

He went to take the advantage of a silent evening and a solitary field for meditation and prayer, those divine exercises by which we converse with God and our own hearts . . . Holy souls love retirement. It will do us good to be often left alone, walking alone and sitting alone; and, if we have the art of improving solitude, we shall find we are never less alone than when alone. Meditation and prayer ought to be both our business and our delight when we are alone (Henry, *Commentary on the Whole Bible*, 43).

Now let's look at the example of the apostle Peter: "And on the next day, as they were on their way, and approaching the city, Peter went up on the housetop about the sixth hour to pray" (Acts 10:9). The sixth hour was around noon, and Peter chose a private place to pray. Maybe the breeze was cooler on the roof. There might have been a quiet garden and fountain there or a shade. Above all, it was a place of solitude. So Peter left family members and guests on the ground floor and went up to meet God.

Consider some of the places Jesus chose to talk to His Father. Look first at Matthew's account and then at Mark's:

> And after He had sent the multitudes away, He went up to the mountain by Himself to pray; and when it was evening, He was there alone (Matthew 14:23).

> And immediately He made the disciples get into the boat and go ahead of Him to the other side to Bethsaida, while He Himself was sending the multitude away. And after bidding them farewell, He departed to the mountain to pray (Mark 6:45–46).

Jesus had sent His disciples to Bethsaida. He wanted time alone with His Father. He chose the peace and quiet of a mountain spot. If you have ever prayed on the side of a mountain, you personally know the solitude Jesus experienced. How interesting to see God the Son favoring certain locations of His own creation!

Luke records another occasion of prayer: "And it was at this time that He went off to the mountain to pray, and He spent the whole night in prayer to God" (Luke 6:12).

## JESUS CHOSE LONELY PLACES

Luke emphasizes the humanity of Jesus. The frequent mention of Jesus' prayers evidently had that purpose in view. Since the God-man continued all night in prayer, who is there among us that does not need to continue steadfastly in prayers?

Frank L. Cox wrote: "Every great undertaking in our lives should be preceded by a season of solitude and prayer. This will assure us of God's presence and power in our undertaking" (James Burton Coffman, *Luke* [A.C.U. Press: Abilene, TX, 1975], 119).

Luke says, "And some eight days after these sayings, it came about that He took along Peter, John, and James, and went up to the mountain to pray" (Luke 9:28). What mountain? The Mount of Transfiguration. There Jesus' appearance changed as He was praying (Luke 9:29). His three disciples saw and heard Him talking to Moses and Elijah. Once again Jesus chose a mountain, a secluded spot, to pray. His transfiguration was only seen by the three that accompanied Him.

We see our Savior on several occasions throughout His ministry retreating to a secluded spot to talk to His Father: "But He Himself would often slip away to the wilderness and pray" (Luke 5:16).

Literally, the word for "wilderness" here is "lonely places." It was customary for Christ to slip away from the pressing people and pray in a lonely place, a deserted place. Oh, how He must have treasured these times of quiet in His stressful, short life on earth! Burton Coffman says, "The reliance of Jesus upon God, and His constant dependence upon the Father's will appear throughout the New Testament in the vigorous pursuit of prayer which marked His holy life" (Coffman, *Luke*, 105).

Notice something else from this verse. Jesus frequently stole away from the pressing crowds, the constant needs, and the demands of teaching. Any one of these by itself is stressful enough. It is no wonder that Jesus often sought peace and quiet. In today's language, He had a grueling schedule, mentally and physically exhausting. His earthly ministry afforded Him no time for general rest and relaxation. His time was short and full of stress.

> Jesus frequently stole away from the pressing crowds, the constant needs, and the demands of teaching.

Think of the time that Jesus got into a boat and promptly fell asleep (Mark 4:36–39). Did He fall asleep due to the sheer exhaustion of His mission? Haven't we experienced that same kind of exhaustion when we collapse on our sofa after a horrid day? Retreating to the mountains to talk to His Father was Jesus' lifeline. Escaping on a fishing boat was therapy; these retreats helped Him to stay the course.

## Find Your Quiet Spot

May I add some personal thoughts here? Find your quiet spot. You may have several, as I do. To me, the ocean is the most wonderful place that I know of where I can find God. The sea is soothing and calming to my soul, as I watch the waves ebb and flow. A mountain stream secluded by trees offers prayer opportunities, too. God's majesty surrounds our very being every single day of our life—wherever we are. The Father has seen to it that there are many places that offer refuge from the noisy pressures of everyday living.

Let's see what Matthew Henry, a commentary writer from the 1700s, said about those who find a deserted place to pray: "They will find themselves never less alone than when thus alone . . . A desert is no desert if we be with Christ there" (Henry, *Commentary on the Whole Bible*, 1427). What a sweet, sweet thought!

# HELP!

What if we cannot retire to a quiet place? Do we still pray? Of course we do. I would love to be able to walk right out to the ocean and have a talk with the Lord, but I don't live at the ocean. When I need to go to the Lord immediately, my Begging Place is my walk-in closet. I am able to lie face down and prostrate myself—my begging posture. God gave us powerful minds that enable us to move our spirit to a quiet place, even when our bodies are in a crowd. We can always close our eyes, calm our spirits with the image of our quiet place, and meet Him there.

Many of our prayers are short and brief. That's fine, too. Who hasn't prayed before an exam at school, or before a confrontation with a coworker, or even before calling Visa about a credit card problem? (I even pray for items to be on sale when I go shopping.) Our lives naturally are full of problems, but Christian lives should be full of prayers. Anytime and anywhere. Don't limit God's power—or the power of prayer.

> When we pray for others, we learn to take the focus from our own problems and see the needs of others.

Try keeping a daily prayer journal. Write down your prayers. Find a secluded place that brings you closer to the Creator. Pray while you exercise. I personally have found walking and praying to be fabulous together. You not only are getting in shape physically, but you are also getting fit spiritually. Forget the iPod!

If you have a favorite friend to pray with, do so—a lot! Praying together strengthens the bond between you, as it bonds you both to the Lord. Many friends pray over the phone. I have done so many times when a friend or family member called for help. Many ladies' Bible classes spend much time in prayer. Prayer adds a new dimension to our relationships with sisters.

## HELPFUL HINTS

*Find opportunities for quick prayers.* Pray while standing in the checkout line, driving your car, waiting to pick up your children at school, and while on hold on the telephone. Use extra time wisely. You will be surprised how many everyday opportunities are presented to you for spiritual reconnecting. Learn to "pray without ceasing" (1 Thessalonians 5:17).

✠ *Be ready to pray.* When opportunities arise, stop and pray. Make a list of things for which you should pray and constantly revise it: the church, Christians all over the world, leaders, enemies, peace, families, deacons, elders, ministers, missionaries, strength, courage, and wisdom. Put your list on your mirror; pray as you fix your face and your hair. (How often is this? Daily!) When we pray for others, we learn to take the focus from our own problems and see the needs of others, which opens the door of service for us. When we serve, we are happier. God knows this—He is waiting for us to discover it!

✠ *Use insomnia for prayer time.* Do you have trouble falling asleep? Or do you sometimes awaken in the wee hours of the morning, unable to go back to sleep? (If not, as you grow older, you will.) Use these times for the Lord. Pray about everything on your heart. Ask Him to bless your loved ones. Ask Him to bless your spiritual family—especially new Christians. Pray for opportunities to teach the gospel to lost souls. Put the names of those for whom you are praying before His mighty throne—the sick, troubled, or dying. Ask God to comfort the afflicted. Pray for the day that is dawning. Ask God to bless that day for Him and ask Him for "smooth sailing." Learn to pray about big things and small things.

✠ *Set a time to pray.* Evidently David prayed every morning: "My voice shalt thou hear in the morning, O Lord; in the morning will I direct my prayer unto thee, and will look up" (Psalm 5:3 KJV). Charles Hodge made the following comments on Psalm 5:3 in one of his sermons:

> Does God expect to hear from me every day? Yes, daily. Praying daily does not require a PhD or a high IQ. About 5:00 A.M., God might be saying, "Well, it is about time for ole Hodge to be calling." Begin the day with God. Meet with God before meeting man. Solve today's problems before you run into them. When I get up in the morning, I look for God—for what He is doing in my life—because I want to be in on it. Give God control of the day, or Satan will take it.

Bring God in; He will find His way out. Have a time. Have a place. Meet with God.

## NO TIME

I knelt to pray but not for long,
I had too much to do.
I had to hurry and get to work,
For bills would soon be due.

So I knelt and said a hurried prayer,
And jumped up off my knees.
My Christian duty was now done,
My soul could rest at ease.

All day long I had no time
To spread a word of cheer.
No time to speak of Christ to friends,
They'd laugh at me I feared.

No time, no time, too much to do,
That was my constant cry;
No time to give to souls in need,
But at last the time to die.

And when before the Lord I came,
I stood with downcast eyes.
For in His hands God held a book;
It was the book of Life.

God looked into His book and said,
"Your name I cannot find.
I once was going to write it down—
But never found the time."

—Author unknown

## A HEART CONDITION

Here is one of the saddest verses in the Bible: "And the Lord was sorry that He had made man on the earth, and He was grieved in His heart" (Genesis 6:6).

Does God really have a heart? Oh, not one with an aorta and chambers. But He does have one with deep emotion that can be felt. We are made in His image (Genesis 1:26) so we can grieve His heart. How tragic is the message in Genesis 6:6. How sad to think the Creator regretted making mankind! Imagine God's saying, "Oh, how I wish that I had never created her!" How sad.

> "God sees not as man sees, for man looks at the outward appearance, but the Lord looks at the heart."

God desires that we think properly and have a heart that wants to obey Him in all things. Here is an important admonition from the Father: "And you shall love the Lord your God with all your heart and with all your soul and with all your might" (Deuteronomy 6:5).

Is there anything left of a human after you take away the heart, soul, and might? No. God has always desired that we love Him completely, the same way that He loves us.

Our Father knows us through and through. He is not fooled by our ways or actions; He knows what we are really thinking. The old saying, "you cannot run, you cannot hide," is an apt warning of God's omniscience, His omnipresence, and His omnipotence. Just read Psalm 139, and you will see what I mean.

Listen to what the Lord said to Samuel as he was looking for the proper son of Jesse to anoint as king of Israel:

> Do not look at his appearance or at the height of his stature, because I have rejected him; for God sees not as man sees, for man looks at the outward appearance, but the Lord looks at the heart (1 Samuel 16:7).

The Lord can read our hearts. He knows what we are thinking while we pray. Is it possible to pray in such a way that God is insulted? Oh, yes. Can we pray in such a way that God is displeased with us? Yes, we can. Can we pray with the wrong kind of heart? Of course.

> Take care, brethren, lest there should be in any one of you an evil, unbelieving heart, in falling away from the living God. But encourage one another day after day, as long as it is still called "Today," lest any one of you be hardened by the deceitfulness of sin (Hebrews 3:12–13).

The Hebrews writer was inspired by the Holy Spirit to admonish his readers not to have a heart of unbelief that could result in falling away from the faith. A heart that does not trust in God is an evil heart. And an evil heart is doomed for disaster, because Satan has a foothold on that soul.

## THE PHARISEES' HEART PROBLEM

When the Scribes and Pharisees came asking why Jesus' disciples did not wash their hands before they ate, He addressed their heart problem. These so-called religious men were more concerned with their exaggerated man-made traditions than with keeping God's law. Jesus responded to them:

> You hypocrites, rightly did Isaiah prophesy of you, saying, "This people honors Me with their lips, but their heart is far away from Me. But in vain do they worship Me, teaching as doctrines the precepts of men." And after He called the multitude to Him, He said to them, "Hear, and understand. Not what enters into the mouth defiles the man, but what proceeds out of the mouth, this defiles the man" . . . And He said, "Are you also still lacking in understanding also? Do you not understand that everything that goes into the mouth passes into the stomach, and is eliminated? But the things that proceed out of the mouth come from the heart, and those defile the man. For out of the heart come evil thoughts, murders, adulteries, fornications, thefts, false witness, slanders. These are the things which defile the man; but to eat with unwashed hands does not defile the man" (Matthew 15:7–20).

The hearts of the hypocritical Pharisees were rotten to the core. They were consumed with being pious and dedicated to God, but inside they were full of hatred, envy, and injustice. They worshiped their own laws and traditions to the point that they became arrogant, greedy, and judgmental.

## Holy Act–Rotten Insides

How does this relate to prayer? God knows our hearts. He knows whether or not our supplications are real. He also knows what sort of lives we are living and whether or not they are acceptable. If our lives are full of sin and our hearts are impenitent, God does not hear our prayers. They are empty and vain and useless if we are rotten inside and try to act holy. Let's look at two passages, one from the Old Testament and one from the New Testament:

> Hear the word of the Lord, you rulers of Sodom; give ear to the instruction of our God, you people of Gomorrah. "What are your multiplied sacrifices to Me?" says the Lord. "I have had enough of burnt offerings of rams, and the fat of fed cattle. And I take no pleasure in the blood of bulls, lambs, or goats. When you come to appear before Me, who requires of you this trampling of My courts? Bring your worthless offerings no longer, incense is an abomination to Me. New moon and Sabbath, the calling of assemblies—I cannot endure iniquity and the solemn assembly. I hate your new moon festivals and your appointed feasts, they have become a burden to Me. I am weary of bearing them. So when you spread out your hands in prayer, I will hide My eyes from you, yes, even though you multiply prayers, I will not listen. Your hands are covered with blood" (Isaiah 1:10–15).

> *"I will hide My eyes from you, yes, even though you multiply prayers, I will not listen."*

> If therefore you are presenting your offering at the altar, and there remember that your brother has something against you, leave your offering there before the altar, and go your way; first be reconciled to your brother, and then come and present your offering (Matthew 5:23–24).

What is God saying in these passages? That our hearts must be clean and right before we can pray or offer anything to Him. We have to get our lives right before He will listen to us, help us, or accept our worship.

## WRONG MOTIVES

The brother of Jesus said, "You do not have because you do not ask. You ask and do not receive, because you ask with wrong motives, so that you may spend it on your pleasures" (James 4:2–3).

> Our prayers are often about what we want, not about what God wants.

How often have we prayed and not received an answer? Quite a few times, most likely. Our prayers are often about what we want, not about what God wants. We are sometimes bold enough to set a timetable for God. We ask amiss because our motives are selfish. James is telling his readers that surrender to the Father's will is the important thing, not personal pleasures.

King David was "a man after God's own heart," and yet his sin with Bathsheba caused him great sorrow and guilt. David had enjoyed a very close relationship with the Father and had been mightily blessed and delivered by God. In the Penitent Psalm, Psalm 51, David asked God over and over for forgiveness:

> Create in me a clean heart, O God, and renew a steadfast spirit within me. Do not cast me away from Thy presence, and do not take Thy Holy Spirit from me. Restore to me the joy of Thy salvation, and sustain me with a willing spirit. Then I will teach transgressors Thy ways, and sinners will be converted to Thee . . . For Thou dost not delight in sacrifice, otherwise I would give it; Thou art not pleased with burnt offering. The sacrifices of God are a broken spirit; a broken and a contrite heart, O God, thou wilt not despise (Psalm 51:10–17).

## SIBLING RIVALRY IN GOD'S FAMILY

God expects His children to get along with one another, but do not be surprised when sibling rivalry erupts in the family of God. However, when conflict does arise, we must try to remedy it. If a brother or sister refuses to resolve the problem, we know we have done all we can. God's Word says, "If possible, so far as it depends on you, be at peace with all men" (Romans 12:18).

Note the words "if possible." God understands that peace is not always possible. This passage further says, "So far as it depends on you." We have to do all we can. We must make amends—make the peace, if that is possible.

> Wash yourselves, make yourselves clean; remove the evil of your deeds from My sight. Cease to do evil, learn to do good; seek justice, reprove the ruthless; defend the orphan, plead for the widow. "Come now, and let us reason together," says the Lord. "Though your sins are as scarlet, they will be as white as snow; though they are red like crimson, they will be like wool. If you consent and obey, you will eat the best of the land; but if you refuse and rebel, you will be devoured by the sword" (Isaiah 1:16–20).

We must try to mend broken relationships before we approach God's throne. How can we hope to worship properly when we are at odds with our family? Is your heart right with God? If not, do what it takes to make it right. You will never be sorry.

## THOUGHTS TO PONDER

1. What is a showy prayer?

2. Why would Jesus urge us to pray in an inner room?

3. List some of your favorite places to pray.

4. What should we do if we have a problem with a brother or sister?

## SONG FOR TODAY

### DID YOU THINK TO PRAY?

> Ere you left your room this morning,
> Did you think to pray?
> In the name of Christ our Savior,
> Did you sue for loving favor,
> As a shield today?

> When your heart was filled with anger,
> Did you think to pray?
> Did you plead for grace, my brother,
> That you might forgive another
> Who had crossed your way?

When sore trials came upon you,
Did you think to pray?
When your soul was bowed in sorrow,
Balm of Gilead did you borrow
At the gates of day?

Chorus: O how praying rests the weary!
Prayer will change the night to day;
So when life seems dark and dreary,
Don't forget to pray.

## PRAYER FOR TODAY

*Our Father, we thank You from the bottom of our hearts for giving us life. Thank You for Your care and for the hedge You keep around us. How blessed we are to be called Your children and to have You as our Father! We adore You and magnify Your wondrous name throughout all the earth.*

*Help us to keep our slates clean with You. May our prayers be sincere and heartfelt. Please help us to find more time for spiritual things—for reading Your Word; for talking to You. Help us to focus on You, Your Son, and Your Spirit. Give us peace, O Lord, in this world of stress and sin. Help us to learn to take advantage of quiet places that help us to draw near to You.*

*Thank You, God, for the Holy Spirit. Thank You for Jesus who pleads on our behalf before You. Forgive us when we do wrong and cause You pain. We love You. In Jesus' name. Amen.*

# Becky's Memories

## Mission Field Blessings

One of the most comforting aspects of Christianity is the knowledge that God always keeps His promises. If He says He will bless us on certain conditions, He carries through. Having been raised in a mission field, I experienced firsthand God's promises:

> Jesus said, "Truly I say to you, there is no one who has left house or brothers or sisters or mother or father or children or farms, for My sake and for the gospel's sake, but that he shall receive a hundred times as much now in the present age, houses and brothers and sisters and mothers and children and farms, along with persecutions; and in the age to come, eternal life" (Mark 10:29–30).

Time after time, our family experienced the Father's blessings as He opened the windows of heaven and poured bountiful blessings on us as we worked in New England. We missed our friends, relatives, and brethren in Texas and Oklahoma. But we soon realized the biggest blessing: our family was growing closer to each other. We were all we had. The church was very small. There were no Christians at our school and few youth fellowships. We had to stick together. Our love for each other grew by leaps and bounds. More blessings followed: God protected us from harm, we lacked for nothing, and we were supported by generous brethren.

However, the road was not always smooth. Many times our lives seemed uncertain. Sometimes we didn't know what our next step should be. But the faith of my parents grew stronger and stronger as they learned to walk by faith and not by sight. They, in turn, taught us children to do the same. My parents prayed constantly, many times all night long. We prayed together as a family, too. We shared the same spirit of the mission to be accomplished.

Mom and Dad moved to New England as vocational missionaries. They wanted to help in the mission field simply by being a strong Christian family. We lived in Brattleboro, Vermont, for two years before God led us to full-time mission work. My parents heard of a young Christian nursing student in Concord, New Hampshire, who had no way of attending worship. There was no church in Concord. So we started traveling to Manchester, New Hampshire, where the George Baker family was working. We spent Saturday nights with them and then worshiped in Concord with Ann Leavitt, the nurse, on Sundays. Mom and Dad soon decided to move to Concord.

Concord was a significant city, the capital of New Hampshire. We offered prayers to our Father continually, as Mom and Dad sought His will. Was this the right thing to do? How would we live? Who would support us? The "Macedonian call" was loud and clear. With God's hand leading us, our family moved to Concord and worked there eleven years. Dad was a closet architect; he erected his first church building in Concord.

There was a short hiatus for Mom and Dad in La Grange, Texas, where Dad preached and built another church building. But a funny thing happens when you live in New England. You can never get it out of your blood. Don't even bother trying. Mom and Dad could not wait to return to the Northeast, and God once again led them to their next adventure: the White Mountains of New Hampshire. Surrounded by these beautiful mountains and with majestic Mount Washington in the distance, Mom and Dad established the church and erected a building in Conway, New Hampshire. This was their last work in New England before retiring to Georgia.

Mom often read Mark 10:29–30 and pointed out the words: "along with persecutions." We personally experienced many persecutions, not only from the world but also from the church. Life on any mission field is filled with the good, the bad, and the ugly. Satan packs his little suitcase and travels with the missionary. He sometimes manages to wreak havoc with the lives of missionaries. Our family prayed constantly together, and God showed us the way over and over. We met God at the Begging Place many times, and He never forsook us. God was working in our lives, constantly demonstrating to us His love and guidance. Satan wanted to defeat us and devour us, but God was bigger. Mom often quoted: "Greater is He who is in you than he who is in the world" (1 John 4:4). (Becky's translation: God is bigger than Satan, and He will win every time.)

One of the most wonderful things God did for us was to see that my parents had a retirement income. After thirty years as missionaries, their supporting congregation in Franklin, Tennessee, continued their generous support. They took care of my parents and saw to their every need. What comfort that was to my mother and father, as well as to us children as our parents grew older. Those elders never left my parents' side. They were there offering help when Mom and Dad passed away. They were our rock. They saw all of us through the beginning, the middle, and the end of our tour of duty in New England. Today these men still are committed and involved in converting the lost in the Northeast country.

Our lives were never the same after moving from the Southwest to the Northeast in 1957. We burned our bridges, as Mom often said, and we learned the best formula for mission work: "First a friend, then a brother." Would we do it all over again? In a heartbeat!

Oh, God our Father, thank You for allowing us to go and do mission work. Thank You for all the blessings You poured upon our heads and Your constant presence in our lives. We were, above all families, most blessed!

To our New England brothers and sisters, we say again to you our favorite phrase: "We will see you in heaven—in the northeast corner!"

MOM AND DAD

## CHAPTER 9

# ESTHER THE QUEEN

"If you remain silent at this time,
relief and deliverance will arise for the
Jews from another place and you
and your father's house will perish.
And who knows whether you have not
attained royalty for such a time as this?"
Then Esther told them to reply to Mordecai,
". . . thus I will go in to the king . . .
and if I perish, I perish" (Esther 4:14–16).

The life of Esther is one of the most intriguing in the Old Testament. Esther is a Persian name which means star. Hadassah, her Jewish name, means myrtle. Myrtle was a large evergreen shrub with sweet smelling flowers. Myrtle twigs were often used for making crowns or wreaths.

Esther's story has been told countless times, especially to young Christian girls. Her life personified romance, mystery, humor, danger, and courage. Stop and consider this: if Esther had not pleaded for the lives of Jews, the story of Jesus would be told without her. But thank God, this young girl was used in a masterful way by God to prepare the way for the Messiah.

## WHERE IS GOD?

God's name is never mentioned in the book of Esther. However, His presence is obvious. Why is His name not there? There must have been certain dangers for the Jews when this book was written. Remember, Mordecai had warned Esther not to reveal her nation or kindred when she was taken to the king's house (Esther 2:10). Mordecai had his reasons for so instructing Esther. It is very likely he had had confrontations with Haman, his political enemy.

Although God is not mentioned by name in the book of Esther, every word breathes His sovereignty and providence. Ahasuerus occupied the throne of Persia, but God sat on the throne of heaven . . . The scepter of Ahasuerus was on loan from God, and his regal attire was the robe of a steward (Chesser, *Portrait of God*, 205–206).

## ESTHER'S PURPOSE

Where is the setting of this book? Esther and Mordecai lived in Susa (Shushan), the winter capital for the Persian kings, located near the Persian Gulf in Iran.

What is the purpose of the book? Jews today remember Esther at the yearly feast of Purim. Esther's story reveals how the lot— "pur"—was cast. She is remembered for her role in delivering the nation of Israel. The book's theme is familiar: God uses ordinary people to accomplish His purpose.

> God uses ordinary people to accomplish His purpose.

As Christians, we remember Esther because of her faith in God, her obedience to Him, and her willingness to lay down her life for her people. We see Esther for only about five years, and then she vanishes from Scripture. However, she played an important role in preparing the way for the Messiah. Esther will be remembered forever.

## WHO WAS KING AHASUERUS?

The story of Esther begins with the introduction of Ahasuerus, king of Persia—Xerxes was his Greek name—who ruled the largest empire of the then-known world. He reigned for twenty years (485–465 B.C.). He was volatile and impulsive. Herodotus, the famed Greek historian, recorded several events that reveal huge character flaws in him:

> Greek and Roman historians tell us that Xerxes was a luxurious, voluptuous, and extremely cruel tyrant. After his whole army of 1,040,000 men had been entertained on their march to Greece, and after an enormous sum had been contributed to help defray the cost of that expedition by Pythias, the rich Lydian, Xerxes was so enraged by a request of Pythias, whose five sons were in Xerxes'

army, that the eldest be released to aid the comfort of Pythias' declining years; after all that, Xerxes was so enraged by the request that he ordered Pythias' oldest son to be cut in two, and made his whole army to pass between the pieces.

He even beheaded the men who had built the famous bridge of boats across the Hellespont, because a storm had destroyed it; and he commanded the sea to be scourged, and to be chained by sinking fetters in it! Just imagine old Xerxes whipping the ocean! He was a debauchee who, after his return from Greece, sought to drive away his vexation at this shameful defeat by reveling in the sensual pleasures of his harem (C. F. Keil quotes Herodotus. James Burton Coffman, *Ezra, Nehemiah, Esther* [A.C.U. Press: Abilene, TX, 1993], 306–307).

## VASHTI – DETHRONED!

At the beginning of the book of Esther, Xerxes was planning a military campaign with his princes and military officers, an event that lasted 180 days. At the end of his strategy meeting, Xerxes invited all of Susa to a banquet. The palace, with its golden drinking vessels, was ornate.

In those days in Susa, women and men ate separately, so Queen Vashti planned a special banquet for women. After seven days of eating and drinking, the king ordered Vashti to appear before the men to display her beauty. She refused.

What great courage; she obviously knew his temper. Some think she was ordered to appear nude or scantily clothed. Some believe she was either pregnant or had just given birth. Whatever the case, Vashti lost her place as queen.

The story of Esther reads somewhat like the Cinderella fairy tale. Esther was an outsider, chosen by no works of her own to be queen of an empire. But Esther was real. When Vashti refused to appear before the king, the king agreed to sign an edict declaring she was no longer queen. The Bible says nothing about her being executed, just dethroned. But God was at work. He knew the villain Haman was making plans that had to be stopped. So He raised Esther to sit beside the king to thwart Haman's plans.

## CAPTIVE GIRLS IN HAREM

"After these things when the anger of King Ahasuerus had subsided, he remembered Vashti and what she had done and what had been decreed against her" (Esther 2:1). Four years had passed since Vashti had been dethroned. The king had returned from war. A royal edict was publicized throughout the empire, from India to Ethiopia. Beautiful, young, virgins were brought to the royal harem. A queen would be selected to take Vashti's place. Notice the qualifications: beautiful, young, and a virgin. Esther was among the many young ladies to be groomed for one night with the king. Mordecai, Esther's cousin who had cared for her like a father, warned her not to reveal her nationality. Esther listened to Mordecai, whose job was at the king's gate, probably as a records keeper and official for those who had business with the king.

> Imagine a year of oils and lotions and makeup to soften and enhance a variety of skin types.

## ONE YEAR AT THE SPA

God gives us a description of a Persian health spa. Can we women relate to that? We know about oils, perfumes, lotions, and cosmetics. However, I daresay none of us has ever been to a beauty spa for an entire year. One day, maybe, but not one for an entire year! These girls from all over the empire experienced six months with oil of myrrh and six months with spices, perfumes, and cosmetics. Imagine a year of oils and lotions and makeup to soften and enhance a variety of skin types. (I would think these girls had such smooth and oiled skin that they just shot right off their bed sheets!)

Read Esther 2:12–14. How many of these girls really wanted to have one night with the king? These were very young girls, possibly from ten to sixteen years old. Burton Coffman commented:

> Where are there any sadder words than these? One frightful night in the bed with Ahasuerus, and the next morning relegated to the status of concubine, never more to see him, unless called by name; and the odds are that he did not even remember the names of half of them. The text states that there were many of these women (Coffman, *Ezra, Nehemiah, Esther*, 2).

## THE ROYAL CROWN

Esther had no choice but to do as she was told. She "found favor in the eyes of all who saw her." Did God make her beautiful specifically for the purpose of winning the heart of the most powerful man in the world? Not only was Esther exceptionally beautiful, she also had a pleasing personality. She found favor especially with Hegai, the eunuch in charge.

Esther's turn arrived for her night with the king; she captured his heart:

> And the king loved Esther more than all the women, and she found favor and kindness with him more than all the virgins, so that he set the royal crown on her head and made her queen instead of Vashti (Esther 2:17).

Regardless of Xerxes' character, he loved Esther. She found favor and kindness with him—qualities she would desperately need from him in the future.

## HAMAN, THE EVIL VILLAIN

Chapter 3 begins with a bad omen: "After these events King Ahasuerus promoted Haman . . . and established his authority over all the princes who were with him" (Esther 3:1).

After Haman's promotion, the king ordered all the servants at his gate to bow to Haman. When Mordecai refused to do so, his fellow workers asked: "Why are you transgressing the king's command?" Mordecai simply told them he was a Jew. What was Haman demanding that Mordecai refused to give? Worship. Mordecai believed the only object of worship was Jehovah God.

## KILL THE JEWS!

Haman was filled with rage. Furious because of Mordecai's insubordination, he devised a plan to kill all the Jews throughout the empire. He cast lots by throwing dice until he got the exact date that he desired to eliminate Mordecai and his people. That date was almost a year away. But Haman was very sure of himself. He presented his case before the king (Esther 3:8). Haman did not use the word *Jews*. He referred to them as "a certain people scattered and dispersed among the peoples in all the provinces of your kingdom." Haman lied about their loyalty to the king and obtained permission to destroy the entire nation. The evil villain even promised to give ten million dollars to the king's treasuries. Xerxes refused the money, but somehow the knowledge of the money spread across Susa. (Money always talks.)

Haman received the coveted ring of Xerxes and, along with it, all power to write an edict any way he desired to broadcast the impending annihilation of the Jews. The edict went out over all the Persian kingdom.

> One can almost hear the weeping, the wailing, and the moaning that echoed throughout the Persian Empire.

A scene of huge contrast ends the third chapter of Esther. As the edict was read and posted in Susa, Haman and Xerxes sat down to drink together. The capital city was in chaos. How callous and hard-hearted to be able to relax and drink together after decreeing the deaths of millions! A human life meant nothing to either of them. However, Xerxes had no idea he had just condemned his wife to death. He was not a happy king when he discovered he had been fooled by his right-hand man.

## WAILING OF MORDECAI

I cannot imagine the agony and desperation every Jew must have felt upon learning he had eleven months to live. One can almost hear the weeping, the wailing, and the moaning that echoed throughout the Persian Empire.

Mordecai knew he must attract Queen Esther's attention. He put on sackcloth and ashes and went into the middle of Susa, wailing loudly and bitterly. Esther's eunuchs and maidens informed her of his behavior.

Hathach, Esther's dependable eunuch, was her "go between." Mordecai gave him a copy of the edict and reported Haman's ten-million-dollar bribe. Time and action were of essence. Mordecai did not say, "Wouldn't it be nice if you went to the king?" The Bible says Mordecai ordered her to go to the king and beg for the Jews.

It did not matter to Mordecai that Esther was the most powerful woman in Persia. She was still Hadassah, his cousin. He was her father figure; there was no time for her to quibble or argue. The dastardly edict was already in place. A new law must be made, and all of Persia had to be informed.

## FAITH OF ESTHER AND MORDECAI

A flurry of notes probably flew back and forth between Mordecai and Esther. When Esther realized she needed an audience with her husband, she was hesitant and frightened. The king's failure to extend his golden scepter to an uninvited guest was an order to kill the intruder immediately. Esther was reluctant.

> Then Mordecai told them to reply to Esther, "Do not imagine that you in the king's palace can escape any more than all the Jews. For if you remain silent at this time, relief and deliverance will arise for the Jews from another place and you and your father's house will perish. And who knows whether you have not attained royalty for such a time as this?" Then Esther told them to reply to Mordecai, "Go, assemble all the Jews who are found in Susa, and fast for me; do not eat or drink for three days, night or day. I and my maidens also will fast in the same way. And thus I will go in to the king, which is not according to the law; and if I perish, I perish." So Mordecai went away and did just as Esther had commanded him (Esther 4:13–17).

## PREPARE FOR THE MISSION

Mordecai showed great insight when he told Esther: "Relief and deliverance will arise for the Jews from another place." Although the word *God* is not in the book of Esther, His presence is in these words. Mordecai was telling Esther that God would deliver His people even if she refused to intervene. What a deep faith! And he reminded her that she perhaps had become queen for the express purpose of delivering their people. They both realized death was at their door whether Esther talked to the king with or without an invitation. What did she have to lose?

Esther understood what had to be done, but she was very wise. She did not immediately have a heart-to-heart discussion with the king. First, she instructed Mordecai to unite the Jews in Susa on her behalf. Her plea was not for all citizens—just God's people. Her people.

"Fast for me," said Esther. Why? Because Esther knew her words and actions had to be perfect in order to obtain the king's favor. She had to use extreme wisdom as she revealed the evil plans of the king's right-hand man.

The presence of God is in the word *fast*. To do without food usually brings a person to his knees. Esther asked for more. Her request took fasting to a higher level—a total focus on the crisis at hand. The Jews were to fast and not drink anything for three days. Imagine the number of prayers offered in her behalf during those three days. Esther held the keys to their survival.

> How do you beg for your life? What do you say? You say everything that you feel and need. Your soul is bared.

Were more powerful and touching words ever spoken: If I die, I die? Esther knew what she had to do, and she did it. There was no looking back—only forward. She went into the king's presence, laying her life on the line.

Esther had always been an obedient daughter to Mordecai, but the table was turned. Chapter 4 ends with Mordecai's obeying Esther's command. Not only did she order Mordecai to fast, but she gave similar orders to all the Jews in her hometown.

## THE BEGGING PLACE

How do you beg for your life? What do you say? You say everything that you feel and need. You pour your heart out at the feet of the Father. Your soul is bared. There are no secrets. Those who have heard a doctor say "It is terminal" or "We've done all we can" know what I am talking about. Your prayers are earnest and sincere.

When you go to the Begging Place, you go with a heavy heart and many tears. Maybe an enormous problem or crisis is burdening you. These problems are all-consuming. They are with you when you wake up, all during the day, and when you sleep. Occasionally, the problem is life threatening, just as Esther's was.

What kind of prayers did Esther pray during those three days? She must have prayed about what to say to Xerxes and how to say it. Her burden was exceedingly heavy, for many lives were at stake—men, women, and children. She no doubt offered tearful pleas to the God of Israel for the deliverance of her people.

## Esther's Entrance

The scene that opens chapter 5 is spectacular. The period of fasting, praying, and weeping has come to an end. In case you are wondering what our beautiful Esther wore for this occasion, the Lord has already told us:

> Esther put on her royal robes and stood in the inner court of the king's palace in front of the king's rooms, and the king was sitting on his royal throne in the throne room, opposite the entrance to the palace (Esther 5:1).

Did she put on her crown? I think she played all her royal aces—the robe, the crown, the whole outfit that normally adorned the one and only queen. When Xerxes saw her, he saw the prized beauty of a very long search.

What was going on in Esther's mind as she stood waiting? Surely there was something in her eyes that intrigued Xerxes, this king who certainly knew women. How did her three-day abstinence from food and water affect her appearance? Was her face pale? Perhaps as he gazed at her, the king thought of the day she had become his queen.

According to the Apocrypha—ancient, non-inspired books—Esther fainted when the king extended his scepter. The king then scooped her up in his arms. Now that's romantic—not inspired but romantic!

## What Is Your Request

The king extended his golden scepter to Esther. The event unfolds: "What is troubling you, Queen Esther? And what is your request? Even to half of the kingdom it will be given to you" (Esther 5:3).

Esther wisely waited another day and another banquet before revealing Haman's deadly plot. Haman then found himself begging for his life, kissing the feet of a Jewess. How the tables had turned on him. The king hanged Haman's body on the gallows Haman had built at his own house for Mordecai!

Esther saved her people, and her courageous act is still remembered by all who know the Scriptures.

## FOR YOU AND ME

Esther went to the Begging Place for you and me, even though she did not realize it. As Christians, we claim that promise: "See how great a love the Father has bestowed upon us, that we should be called children of God; and such we are" (1 John 3:1).

> The Begging Place was Esther's first place to go in a time of despair.

The Begging Place was Esther's first place to go in a time of despair. What a powerful lesson for Christians when crises and troubles arise. Not only should we follow her example, we should teach it to our children.

Esther, I look forward to meeting you and talking with you. Thank you for your prayers. Thank you for going to the Begging Place. Thank you for your willingness to die for your people—and mine. You are a true sister.

And thank you, Father, for showing us women that we can accomplish powerful things for God.

## FOR SUCH A TIME AS THIS

The lovely Queen of Persia sat upon her lofty throne,
Wrestling with a decision that she had to make alone.

The Jews, her native people, were about to be destroyed,
And Queen Esther must revoke the law and try to make it void.

She knew if she went before the King, that she could surely die,
But her mind kept lingering on the words of Mordecai.

He revealed to her the evil plot and told her of the risks,
"You may have been made Queen," he said, "for such a time as this."

And so with faith and courage, Esther knew what she must do.
"If I perish, I perish," she bravely said, and she saved her fellow Jews.

Now, you may not have to risk your life to show how much you care,
But perhaps you face a problem that seems difficult to bear.

Your faith is being tested, and your life seems all amiss,
It could be God has brought you here for such a time as this.

Or maybe you must speak against an evil you have seen,
But you fear for what might happen if you try to intervene.

Just do whatever you must do to uphold righteousness,
And God will help and strengthen you for such a time as this.

—Tami Coble Brown

## THOUGHTS TO PONDER

1. What is the most amazing characteristic of the book of Esther?

2. Describe the character of Xerxes.

3. What role does Mordecai play in this book?

4. Tell of the irony in Haman's ordering a gallows built for Mordecai.

## SONG FOR TODAY

### GREAT IS THY FAITHFULNESS

Great is Thy faithfulness, O God my Father;
There is no shadow of turning with Thee;
Thou changest not, Thy compassions, they fail not;
As Thou hast been, Thou forever wilt be.

Pardon for sin and a peace that endureth,
Thine own dear presence to cheer and to guide;
Strength for today and bright hope for tomorrow,
Blessings all mine, with ten thousand beside!

Chorus: Great is Thy faithfulness!
Great is Thy faithfulness!
Morning by morning new mercies I see.
All I have needed Thy hand hath provided;
Great is Thy faithfulness, Lord, unto me!

## PRAYER FOR TODAY

*Dear God, our hearts rejoice because You have given us Your precious Word, the Bible. Thank You for this wondrous and magnificent gift. We are so grateful for the accounts of righteous men and women who lived long ago and bravely sought to please You.*

*Thank you for the marvelous story of Esther and her willingness to die for Your people. Thank You for honoring this woman, Lord. We want to meet her in heaven and talk with her, if that is Your will for us.*

*Please help us women to be strong and courageous, and to stand for what is right, as Esther did. And, Lord, please help us to raise our daughters to have Esther's integrity. Please bless us, O Lord, and send us wherever we can do the most good for You. In Jesus' name. Amen.*

# BECKY'S MEMORIES

## EMERGENCY, EMERGENCY!
## THE DEVIL IS LOOSE!

Everybody has troubles. Even righteous Job said, "For man is born for trouble, as sparks fly upward" (Job 5:7). In short, life is tough.

Satan has again attacked my family. I have already been to the Begging Place twice. This beautiful, sunny Saturday has become very stormy, with more inclement weather on the horizon. I am at war with that old devil again. But I know, as sure as I know myself, that my precious Father is watching me and hearing me and delivering all of us.

I remember times of conflict as I grew up in a house of short tempers and often heated words. (No, my parents were not perfect, and yes, I heard them argue!) When my mother got upset with my dad, she called him Ethyl. (He seemed to have an invisible can of gasoline that he used to start little fires of conflict.) As is true with any married couple, Dad knew just the right words to get Mom going—and vice versa.

Satan is pure Ethyl. He gleefully ignites arguments among Christians that burst into fiery catastrophes. He is bent on setting ablaze our marriages and relationships and causing more divorces—or homicides.

Our family is upset today. Jeff and I have already had a little spat in the kitchen. But I must say, it was over quickly; we were back on course in a few minutes. After thirty-three years of marriage, we choose our battles carefully, and this was only a trifling skirmish. Our son Jeffrey, his pregnant wife Angela, and Will, our two-year-old grandson are all trying to move to another town today; we are concerned.

You know about moving, don't you? Statistically, it is rated right up there with divorce and death. (Come to think about it, moving sometimes causes divorce or death!) Jeffrey's plan is to drive a packed U-Haul to our house, with Angela and Will following in the family car. Tomorrow we are to drive to their new home and help them unpack.

That is the plan. Satan—a.k.a. Ethyl—has a plan, too. His plan is to destroy our plan—to conquer and divide.

Jeffrey called. His friends helped him pack the truck yesterday, and they all said their goodbyes. Today this little family set off, and—you guessed it—the truck broke down. They got the truck back to the station, and U-Haul wound up towing it to another town for repairs. Jeffrey is upset; Angela is crying; Will is making cowboy noises.

We try to help them as much as we can, but I feel utterly helpless. I know this feeling well—the feeling a mother experiences when her children are far away, in trouble, and there is absolutely nothing she can do except beg God and cry.

Our daughter Jennifer and her husband Tim are planning to help the movers unpack tomorrow. I called Jennifer—she and Tim were in their favorite Chinese restaurant—and related what had happened. She moaned: "Oh, man, I have heard all of the war stories about U-Haul."

"What have you heard?" I asked.

"I have a friend who went through four trucks before they got to their new home!" Oh, no. Another stomach ulcer!

Jennifer continued, "Listen, Mom, I need to go. This has been an awful day for us, too."

"Why?" I asked.

"Let's just say we are having some major attitude problems," she replied. "Anything that could possibly go wrong has gone wrong."

Yes, Ethyl is alive and well. He has hit all of my family today, including me. But he will not have the last say.

Jeff and I prayed together. Then I went to the Begging Place, the closet, fell down on my face, and boldly entered the throne room of my Father. With worried tears I told Him of the day's events. I told Him how much I loved Him and admitted that He was in charge. I asked for answers and solutions to today's evils. I could not handle all these problems, so I cast them upwards for Him to catch. And I found peace again.

When stressful and exasperating events occur, we can choose either to grow or to grouse. We can holler, squawk, and carry on, or we can turn to the Lord for "help in time of need" (Hebrews 4:16). Learning to lean on the everlasting arms takes time—and tests. Job knew this, too.

Jesus knew there would be times like this. He taught the multitudes: "Therefore do not be anxious for tomorrow: for tomorrow will care for itself. Each day has enough trouble of its own" (Matthew 6:34).

I believe the King James Version translates this passage the best: "Take therefore no thought for the morrow: for the morrow shall take thought for the things of itself. Sufficient unto the day is the evil thereof."

My mother used to say, "The devil's loose!" I would laugh and say, "Mom, stop saying that." I didn't think Satan had that kind of freedom, but I have grown up now. I have seen his evil works first-hand. Mom was absolutely correct. The devil is loose!

But I have also lived long enough to see my Lord in control of all things. Today I am comforting myself with the psalmist's words: "The Lord will accomplish what concerns me" (Psalm 138:8).

What does *accomplish* mean? To complete, achieve, carry out, or fix. The Lord will complete what concerns me. He knows what I am troubled about. He knows what Satan has just thrown in my path. As I have grown older and learned to trust in Him completely, this passage really rings true. He has accomplished. He has completed. I trust in Him completely. My Father will deliver Jeffrey, Angela, and little Will. He will deliver all of us.

Oh yes, the devil's loose. Ethyl is at work, starting fires here and there in my family's life. And he is also seeking someone to devour. Not nibble. Not munch. Devour!

But I will not fear any longer, and I will not worry. I have been to the Begging Place, and my Father will solve our problems and personally handle Ethyl. You see, God is the only one who can.

*(P.S. God provided a new truck; professional packers transferred the cargo; one night was spent at a nearby hotel; all expenses were paid by Jeffrey's boss; church members met the U-Haul truck at the new home, unloaded the truck, and brought food. Jeffrey is smiling; Angela is smiling; Will is still making cowboy noises. Is God wonderful or what?)*

CHAPTER 10

# THE BEST WAY TO PRAY

*But the tax-gatherer, standing some distance away,*
*was even unwilling to lift up his eyes to heaven,*
*but was beating his breast, saying,*
*"God, be merciful to me, the sinner!"*
*I tell you, this man went down to*
*his house justified rather than the other;*
*for everyone who exalts himself shall be humbled,*
*but he who humbles himself shall be exalted*
*(Luke 18:13-14).*

A priest, a minister, and a guru sat discussing the best positions for prayer, while a telephone repairman worked nearby.

"Kneeling is definitely the best way to pray," the priest said.

"No," said the minister. "I get the best results standing with my hands outstretched to heaven."

"You're both wrong," the guru said. "The most effective prayer position is lying down on the floor."

The repairman could contain himself no longer. "Hey fellas," he interrupted. "The best prayin' I ever did was when I was hangin' upside down from a telephone pole!"

Does the Bible tell us we must kneel when we pray or look toward Jerusalem as Daniel did? No. But did you kneel by your bed when you were little? Many of us did. Perhaps you saw your parents kneeling by their bed before they retired. That is the way my parents ended each day.

As a child I observed older men kneeling beside their pews for prayer during worship. I also recall being at my parents' home several years ago and all of us getting on our knees to pray because of a crisis in our family. Kneeling is humbling, bending your knees before the Father. Kneeling is submission. Kneeling is demonstrating to God that you are seeking His face as you make your supplications and requests before Him.

Brother Willie Cato wrote of a lesson he learned from brother Marshall Keeble about kneeling in prayer:

> Brother Keeble and I were in Cleburne, Texas. We spent the night in the home of brother and sister John Featherstone, who had recently returned from a period of service in Nigeria. While brother Keeble was in the bathroom preparing for bed, I turned the cover down on his bed, then turned the cover down on mine and climbed into the bed. When he returned, I was lying in bed, with one leg propped up and the other crossed. He asked, "Son, what are you doing?" I said, "I'm just lying here relaxing and visiting with the Lord." Quickly, brother Keeble asked, "Like that? The Lord ain't going to accept nothing that relaxed. Get up and get out of the bed and let me show you how to pray."
>
> I climbed out of bed, he instructed me to get down on my knees beside the bed, he did the same, and we prayed together. Yes, he was a man of prayer, praying fervently for hours. The disciples of the Lord said "teach us to pray." As a student of Marshall Keeble, I was also taught to pray (Cato, *His Hand and Heart*, 118).

## EXAMPLES OF KNEELING

Study biblical examples of kneeling in prayer and you will be amazed at the many instances of this position. For instance, Daniel 6:10 tells us of Daniel's custom of kneeling and praying three times a day with his face toward Jerusalem.

Here are some Scriptures for your study. In them you will find Solomon, Jesus, Paul, and even some with no name mentioned.

| | | |
|---|---|---|
| 1 Kings 8:54 | Mark 1:40 | Acts 9:40 |
| Luke 22:41 | Mark 10:17 | Daniel 6:10 |
| Matthew 17:14 | Acts 21:5 | |

As we consider these thoughts on kneeling while praying, let us consider a psalm of David:

> Come, let us worship and bow down; let us kneel before the Lord our Maker. For He is our God, and we are the people of His pasture, and the sheep of His hand (Psalm 95:6–7).

There is something about this kneeling. It is bowing our entire body before the Lord as we ask Him to listen to our prayer. It is acknowledging Him as the Supreme Creator and our Father. It is surrendering to His will. Try it. I think God likes it.

## One More Time

O God, please hear my cry.
My heart is broken and my world gone awry.
O God, please answer my plea.
Pour out Your peace and comfort while loving me.
And, please God, this is a must—
Once more remember that I am just dust.

—Becky Blackmon

## Another Intercessor

Did you know we have another intercessor, other than Jesus, when we pray? God in His marvelous love has seen fit to provide the Holy Spirit to intercede for us.

> And in the same way the Spirit also helps our weakness; for we do not know how to pray as we should, but the Spirit Himself intercedes for us with groanings too deep for words; and He who searches the hearts knows what the mind of the Spirit is, because He intercedes for the saints according to the will of God (Romans 8:26–27).

We should not be alarmed when we wonder about our prayer life. Even one of the men who daily walked with the Lord asked Him to teach His disciples to pray. Part of our growth as Christians is a desperate desire that our supplications be proper and pleasing to the Father. We do not want to pray in a wrong manner. If our hearts are right with the Lord, we desire everything else to be right with Him, too.

This is where the Holy Spirit comes in. The Scripture says that He "helps our weakness." Now that is comforting. He knows what we are trying to say to God. Perhaps we are saying it poorly. He takes our words in prayer—our weakness—and speaks in our stead. And the Spirit speaks God's language! He knows just what to say. And God knows what the Spirit is saying because God knows the mind of the Holy Spirit.

The Spirit speaks God's language! He knows just what to say.

As we delve into those passages about Jesus being our High Priest and the Holy Spirit speaking God's language, we realize how much God loves us. Not only did He give us His own Son, but He also gave us a method by which we could talk to Him. He will see to it—by means of Jesus and the Holy Spirit—that He receives our prayers in the right form. What more could the Father do for His children?

## THE RIGHT ATTITUDE

What should be the attitude of the one leading a prayer? Jesus said,

> And whenever you stand praying, forgive, if you have anything against anyone; so that your Father also who is in heaven may forgive you your transgressions. But if you do not forgive, neither will your Father who is in heaven forgive your transgressions (Mark 11:25–26).

All who worship, not just the leader, have an obligation during prayer. My mother once witnessed a nervous young man, easily embarrassed, who was appointed to close worship with prayer. Very shakily he walked to the microphone and led the congregation as best he could. Immediately afterwards an older woman approached and remarked, "Young man, if I couldn't pray better than that, I wouldn't pray at all!" Can you guess what happened? That young man never led another public prayer. Perhaps he never returned to worship. God is not pleased when we sit in critical judgment of leaders who are doing their best. The attitude of one's heart is God's business, not ours.

*The attitude of one's heart is God's business, not ours.*

Christians are our brothers and sisters, faults and all. A wise preacher said, "People need two things: a relationship with God and a relationship with the people of God." Christ died for His family, and we have a responsibility every day to act as Christ would. God is love. Christ is love. The Holy Spirit is love. Can our brothers and sisters say we are love?

## TWO PRAYER PARABLES

During His earthly ministry, Jesus spoke a lot about the aspects of prayer. As He traveled about with His disciples, they probably had many conversations about prayer. Wouldn't you have loved listening in on those lively discussions as they walked the long, dusty roads?

In Luke 18 Jesus told two parables back to back to demonstrate the importance of prayer, the frequency of prayer, God's answering of prayer, and the attitude of prayer. Let's look at these parables:

### THE UNJUST JUDGE

There was in a certain city a judge who did not fear God, and did not respect man. And there was a widow in that city, and she kept coming to him, saying, "Give me legal protection from my opponent." And for a while he was unwilling; but afterward he said to himself, "Even though I do not fear God nor respect man, yet because this widow bothers me, I will give her legal protection, lest by continually coming she wear me out." And the Lord said, "Hear what the unrighteous judge said; now shall not God bring about justice for His elect who cry to Him day and night, and will He delay long over them? I tell you that He will bring about justice for them speedily" (Luke 18:2–8).

Jesus told this parable to "show at all times they ought to pray and not to lose heart." He knew His disciples might become discouraged after He left them, but He also knew they could even become discouraged with their prayer life. Jesus knows we can become discouraged, too. So the lesson is also for us. Don't give up hope. God is listening.

How can we lose heart when we pray? Well, haven't you prayed several times for something, and seemingly, nothing happened? Just keep on praying and don't become discouraged. The Father is listening. Keep your faith and keep praying. God works in His own time.

The irreverent judge in the parable does not represent God. He heard the woman's case because he knew she was not going away. She was at the mercy of this judge, so she persisted. She had no alternative. She was a widow and there was no welfare system for her.

I can identify with the widow. Many times I have had a particular request of God—a plea, an earnest cry for help. My only option was to turn to God over and over and over. He was and is my only hope. Trust me. As a woman, I know how to be persistent! I can be the best "pesterer" in the world. I just continue to pray for the same thing again and again. I know my Father in heaven is hearing my cries. I never give up. The Father will answer my prayer in His time. He is just saying, "Wait a while," or He may be saying, "No!"

David knew how to be persistent. Look at what he wrote: "As for me, I shall call upon God, and the Lord will save me. Evening and morning and at noon, I will complain and murmur, and He will hear my voice" (Psalm 55:16–17).

The lesson Jesus was trying to get across was "not to lose heart." We must be hopeful as we put our requests at God's feet. The Father loves us. He is listening and He will give us an answer.

## THE PHARISEE AND THE PUBLICAN

Two men went up into the temple to pray, one a Pharisee, and the other a tax-gatherer. The Pharisee stood and was praying thus to himself, "God, I thank Thee that I am not like other people: swindlers, unjust, adulterers, or even like this tax-gatherer. I fast twice a week; I pay tithes of all that I get." But the tax-gatherer, standing some distance away, was even unwilling to lift up his eyes to heaven, but beating his breast, saying, "God, be merciful to me, the sinner!" I tell you, this man went down to his house justified rather than the other; for everyone who exalts himself shall be humbled, but he who humbles himself shall be exalted (Luke 18:10–14).

What was Jesus' aim in relating this parable? Verse 9 says He told this to certain ones who were self-righteous and haughty—those who looked upon others with contempt. We all know this type, don't we? This Pharisee was most likely a very educated and wealthy man, but his sect of the Jews was most arrogant. The Pharisees looked down with contempt on the average person; they thought themselves to be superior. Herod was stricken with worms—and died!—because he failed to give God the glory (Acts 12:21–23).

The Pharisee was arrogant and self-absorbed. His prayer had "I" trouble—"I" did this and "I" am not like that. His was not really a prayer but an egotistical presentation to remind God how good and righteous he was. He trusted in himself so much that he saw no need for God's grace.

On the other hand, the publican would not even lift his head to pray to God. With a bowed head and beating on his breast, he made one request: "God, be merciful to me, the sinner!" The publican went home justified—forgiven. He received God's grace.

You can imagine how the crowd reacted to this parable. They disliked publicans, the tax-gatherers, who cheated the people and pocketed the money. And they also were very well acquainted with the pride of the Pharisees. Christ's lesson was simple: If you honor yourself, you will fall. If you humble yourself, you will be forgiven. The conclusion? God hears humble prayers—not arrogant ones.

## A CONTRITE HEART

Have you ever prayed as the publican did? Have you ever begged God for mercy? Have you ever wept as you approached the Father's throne of grace? Listen to the beautiful words of two of David's thought-provoking psalms:

- "The Lord is near to the brokenhearted, and saves those who are crushed in spirit" (Psalm 34:18).

- "For Thou dost not delight in sacrifice, otherwise I would give it; Thou art not pleased with burnt offering. The sacrifices of God are a broken spirit; a broken and a contrite heart, O God, Thou wilt not despise" (Psalm 51:16–17).

What is David saying to us across the centuries? Our disposition must be humble, remorseful, and penitent when we pray. God does not want our sacrifices or our money. He has no need of "things" because He owns the world. He just wants us to have the right kind of hearts, hearts that are broken because of our sins—contrite hearts—because of our failures to do right. Our attitude must be correct as we kneel at our Father's throne or we will not find mercy. Don't we all need mercy? Let us resolve to be humble and penitent. Let us practice bowing our spirits before Him.

## THOUGHTS TO PONDER

1. List three persons in the Bible who knelt in prayer.

2. What kind of trouble did the Pharisee have?

3. Quote a Scripture that shows God loves a penitent heart.

4. Define mercy.

## SONG FOR TODAY

### ON BENDED KNEE

On bended knee I come,
With a humble heart I come;
Bowing down before Your holy throne.
Lifting holy hands to You,
As I pledge my love anew.
I worship You in spirit,
I worship You in truth;
Make my life a holy praise unto You.

On bended knee I come,
With a broken heart I come;
Bowing down before Your holy throne.
As I look upon Your face,
Show Your mercy and Your grace.
Change my life, O Holy Spirit,
Make me fresh and ever new;
Make my life a holy sacrifice to You.

## PRAYER FOR TODAY

*Holy Father, thank You for the beauty of this day, and thank You for giving us another day to live for You. Help us in all things to please You with our words and actions toward others. Please forgive us of our sins today, Lord, and help us to curb our outbursts and learn to just listen. Help us not always to offer advice. Help us to be silent and not prideful.*

*Lord, we beg You to meet us at the Begging Place and remember our sins no more. We know that Jesus and the Holy Spirit tell You when and why our hearts are broken. O God, we know You gave us Jesus to understand what it is like to be here on earth and feel all alone. Thank You for the Holy Spirit, who will speak Your language for us and explain why our lives are upside down. Help us to learn from this experience and to reach out more to those who need help, too.*

*May we start over, O God. Please have mercy on us and give us another chance. We love You so. Help us to find our way home to You. In Jesus' name we pray. Amen.*

# BECKY'S MEMORIES

## THERE IS NO PLACE LIKE GANDERBROOK

Ganderbrook Christian Camp is nestled in Maine's beautiful woodlands. There is no place like it on the face of this earth—there is only one Ganderbrook. Once a fine hunting lodge, it is adequately equipped with cabins, a clay tennis court, a nearby lake, and lots of wide open spaces.

Near the end of the '50s, several men from area churches of Christ formed a Ganderbrook Christian Camp board, purchased this camp, and organized it for youth camping sessions, family spiritual retreats, singles' meetings, men's retreats, and women's retreats. Through the years it has grown and flourished by the loving care of New England Christians.

Being a camper there was a blast! The classes were wonderful; the food was fabulous; new friendships became everlasting; and God was with us. One of the things that stood out for any camper was the Friday night devo. All campers, counselors, and visiting adults, surrounded by the blackest of skies with myriads of stars, formed a huge circle on the softball field and sang, "My God and I."

After leaving for college, I did not return to Ganderbrook until I was a young mother. And that women's retreat was like no other. All six New England states were represented, as well as a few others.

My mom was on the very first planning committee. She spoke at every retreat she could attend. She always told me: "Becky, the women at Ganderbrook are so hungry for teaching. I have never seen anybody like them. They come with empty buckets, and they yearn for spiritual instruction. Many of these women are new Christians with difficult lives, difficult husbands, and difficult children. They are hard workers; they have escaped for a weekend, and they are looking for answers. They are hungry. They hang on every word that is said and fill up their buckets, praying that they can stay strong until next year's meeting. These women are special. If you ever are asked to speak to them, you have been given a great honor, and you must not disappoint them."

There is no place like Ganderbrook. Women put down their crosses and laugh and cry together. It truly is a great honor to speak there. These sisters are unique, loving, and giving. They are honest, open, and blunt about their problems. They are not afraid to open their hearts and bare their souls. But most of all, they want to know how to please God. God blesses Ganderbrook because He knows the hearts of those women.

The air at Ganderbrook is clean and clear, with an aroma of the most wonderful blend of grasses and evergreens. I occasionally get a whiff of that "Ganderbrook scent" in Texas, and my heart stops for a moment. I think God must send me these whiffs from time to time, saying, "Remember Ganderbrook; remember the girls."

Lives are changed at Ganderbrook. Christians become more dedicated and committed to God. Dr. Joe Virone. one of the finest men I have ever known, is a great example. He always had a big smile on his face. In his early forties, he came to camp with Kathy and their two little girls to serve as doctor or janitor, depending on our needs. He had his work cut out for him at the ladies' retreats just keeping the well and the bathrooms in working order.

When we learned Dr. Joe had been diagnosed with cancer, our world stood still. We began immediately to pray for him. He went through chemotherapy treatments, but the cancer remained. Fran, his mother-in-law, told this story at a ladies' retreat:

> Yes, I remember that time at Ganderbrook very well. There were more than three hundred women at the retreat that year. One of the ladies went to the podium to announce Doctor Joe's illness and prognosis. When she asked that we pray, every woman I could see got up and knelt beside her chair. It was awesome! I was overwhelmed with emotion and the women beside me just put their arms around me. I have never seen that before that time or since. I cry now remembering it. God said yes to that prayer and Joe started feeling better that weekend. God gave him one more year to live.

Three hundred women on their knees, begging God for more time for a brother, went to the Begging Place. God heard and answered their fervent prayers. Oh, my friends, it is surely true: there is no place like Ganderbrook.

167

## CHAPTER 11

# A Man after God's Own Heart

And after He had removed him,
He raised up David to be their king,
concerning whom He also testified and said,
'I have found David the son of Jesse,
a man after My heart,
who will do all My will'
(Acts 13:22).

The shepherd king of Israel walked closely with God. No, David was not perfect—far from it. He was a man, and he made many mistakes. The sin with Bathsheba and the murder of her husband Uriah always rush immediately into our minds as we consider the "man after God's own heart." We fail to remember two very important facts: God forgave David and David paid hugely for those sins.

How interesting to note that two of the most quoted Scriptures in the Bible concern David and the word *heart!*

> But the Lord said to Samuel, "Do not look at this appearance or at the height of his stature, because I have rejected him; for God sees not as man sees, for man looks at the outward appearance, but the Lord looks at the heart" (1 Samuel 16:7).

Samuel was at the house of Jesse where God was guiding him to select and anoint the next king of Israel. The process is amusing. Each son is ushered in and Samuel is thinking to himself: *This must be the son that God has chosen to be king.* Seven times God speaks to him and rejects all seven sons. But when David comes in from the field, God tells Samuel he is the one.

God does not view people as we do. The Father looks at the heart, not the outward appearance. We do just the opposite. We make judgment calls based on how people are dressed or the way they talk or how much money they have. If Samuel had had his way, he would have anointed Jesse's oldest son Eliab. However, Eliab was not to be king, David was. David's heart was better than those of his brothers.

## DO ALL MY WILL

Paul described David's heart to worshipers in the synagogue in Antioch: "He raised up David to be their king, concerning whom He also testified and said, 'I have found David the son of Jesse, a man after My heart, who will do all My will'" (Acts 13:22).

David was called a man after God's own heart because he wanted to do everything God had in mind for him to do—plain and simple. We often neglect to read "who will do all My will." It shouts volumes about David's mind-set. God's will was his will. As a result, God blessed him abundantly.

The lesson for us is easy. If we want a close relationship with the Lord like David had, our supreme goal will be to do the Lord's will—plain and simple. And God will bless us abundantly.

## THE BIGGEST MISTAKE OF THEIR LIVES

David made the biggest mistake of his life when he did not go to battle in the spring, as he was accustomed to do. Instead, he sent his men. I have always wondered why he remained in Jerusalem.

Bathsheba made the biggest mistake of her life when she decided to take a bath on the rooftop. It seems she did not take proper precautions, that she was not entirely innocent in exposing herself to David's prying eyes. They were both in the wrong place at the wrong time, and the price for their sin was enormous. Satan was the mastermind here; he set both of them up for a complete fall.

David lusted after her, sent for her, and committed adultery with her. Upon learning she was pregnant, David immediately sent to the battlefield for her husband, Uriah the Hittite, so he could sleep with Bathsheba. Uriah refused to go to his own home, even when David made him drunk. David sent him back to battle with orders to Joab that Uriah be killed. True to the king's orders, Uriah died when his comrades were given a secret order to retreat. Bathsheba mourned her husband (2 Samuel 11:26–27). Then she married David and bore him a son.

On that fateful day when the prophet Nathan visited David and bravely told him "you are the man," David came face to face with himself. He clearly saw his affair with Bathsheba, the cover-up, and the murder of Uriah. He had to be sick to his stomach when he realized what he had done. The law demanded that the two should be stoned, and God's kings were not above the law. But David did not die:

> Then David said to Nathan, "I have sinned against the Lord." And Nathan said to David, "The Lord also has taken away your sin; you shall not die. However, because by this deed you have given occasion to the enemies of the Lord to blaspheme, the child also that is born to you shall surely die" (2 Samuel 12:13–14).

## DAVID GOES TO THE BEGGING PLACE

The account in 2 Samuel describes the immediate actions of King David: "David therefore inquired of God for the child; and David fasted and went and lay all night on the ground" (2 Samuel 12:16). He refused to be comforted until he knew God's will for the child:

> And the elders of his household stood beside him in order to raise him up from the ground, but he was unwilling and would not eat food with them. Then it happened on the seventh day that the child died. And the servants of David were afraid to tell him that the child was dead, for they said, "Behold, while the child was still alive, we spoke to him and he did not listen to our voice. How then can we tell him that the child is dead, since he might do himself harm!" But when David saw that his servants were whispering together, David perceived that the child was dead; so David said to his servants, "Is the child dead?" And they said, "He is dead." So David arose from the ground, washed, anointed himself, and changed his clothes; and he came into the house of the Lord and worshiped. Then he came to his own house, and when he requested, they set food before him and he ate. Then his servants said to him, "What is this thing that you have done? While the child was alive, you fasted and wept; but when the child died, you arose and ate food." And he said, "While the child was still alive, I fasted and wept; for I said, 'Who knows, the Lord may be gracious to me, that the child may live.' But now he has died; why should I fast? Can I bring him back

*They were both in the wrong place at the wrong time. The price for their sin was enormous.*

again? I shall go to him, but he will not return to me" (2 Samuel 12:17–23).

With prayers, tears, and hunger, David went to the Begging Place. He did everything in his power to demonstrate his penitence. He wept with great sorrow as he considered the words of Nathan: "The child also that is born to you shall surely die." His heart was filled with wretched guilt. He had committed adultery, murdered Uriah, and lost his son. With his sin staring him in the face, David must have realized Uriah was truly the better man. But perhaps what hurt David most was that he hurt God. A relationship that David cherished had been critically injured.

> We do not have to understand why God acts as He does.

Seven days and nights of fasting and praying and weeping will mature a person. David was not the same man when he arose that seventh day. He would never be the same again. He had sinned and God had forgiven him, but the death of his child was the first of many consequences that would continue to rise for the rest of his life. He was a sadder but wiser king, but still a "man after God's own heart." Don't forget that.

## DOES GOD ANSWER PRAYER?

Does God answer our prayers? Of course He does. Does God answer our prayers in the manner we want Him to? No. He answers them in the way that is best for us. How important for us to pray that His will be done in all things, even if His will conflicts with ours! Learning to accept His will is part of His formula to develop content and secure Christians. Maturity dictates that we desire God's will and God's ways. We do not have to understand why God acts as He does. Trust is letting go of worldly desires and lusts and letting the Father reign supremely in our lives. We know this one thing to be true: God's way is always the best way.

When David went to the Begging Place, God answered every prayer he offered up. God said yes to the appeal for forgiveness, but God said no to sparing the child's life. No one gets a yes from God every time. An answered prayer is not the same as having our way.

In order to achieve contentment, we must accept God's formula—His will. We think we know what is best for us, but realistically we do not know God's will. We cannot see what is ahead, but God knows. Praying is the threshold of faith and trust. Prayer opens the doors that lead to the Father, and we walk through them by faith. We know what God can do. We pray for wisdom to accept the things we cannot change. We learn to pray as Jesus did in Gethsemane: "Not as I will, but as Thou wilt" (Matthew 26:39).

## PRAYER OF UNKNOWN CONFEDERATE SOLDIER

I asked God for strength, that I might achieve,
I was made weak, that I might learn humbly to obey.
I asked for health, that I might do greater things.
I was given infirmity, that I might do better things.
I asked for riches, that I might be happy,
I was given poverty, that I might be wise.
I asked for power, that I might have the praise of men,
I was given weakness, that I might feel the need of God.
I asked for all things, that I might enjoy life,
I was given life, that I might enjoy all things.
I got nothing that I asked for—but everything I had hoped for.
Almost despite myself, my unspoken prayers were answered.
I am among all men [women], most richly blessed.

## FINDING FORGIVENESS

Have you seen the slogan, "God accepts knee-mail"? We grow up when we are on our knees with our backs against the wall, willing to let Him do what is best. If you have reached that level of maturity, you are close to the Father. Your love for Him has become real and unmoving. You have built your house on the rock. Storms of life blow in vain. On top of all of this, you have inserted another factor into life's equation: When you go to the Begging Place, God will hear your prayers and bless your life because He knows your heart.

David went to the Begging Place as a result of his sin against God. We too must sometimes go to the Begging Place because we have transgressed God's law. I am so thankful He is there waiting for us. As David did, we will find forgiveness and God's will for our lives at the Begging Place.

O Thou who dost hear prayer, to Thee all men come. Iniquities prevail against me; as for our transgressions, Thou dost forgive them. How blessed is the one whom Thou dost choose, and bring near to Thee, to dwell in Thy courts. We will be satisfied with the goodness of Thy house, Thy holy temple (Psalm 65:2–4).

God forgave David, but did David have trouble forgiving himself? Probably. God took away David's sin, but David was left with the memory. Perhaps God wants us to remember sin so we will know its pain and abstain from it. David wrote many songs and psalms that praise our God for His kindness and deliverance. But in Psalm 51, David poured out his heart before the Lord, asking Him to forgive the affair with Bathsheba. Read it aloud and pause and think.

Be gracious to me, O God, according to Thy lovingkindness; according to the greatness of Thy compassion blot out my transgression. Wash me thoroughly from my iniquity, and cleanse me from my sin. For I know my transgressions, and my sin is ever before me. Against Thee, Thee only, I have sinned, and done what is evil in Thy sight, so that Thou art justified when Thou dost speak, and blameless when Thou dost judge. Behold, I was brought forth in iniquity, and in sin my mother conceived me. Behold, Thou dost desire truth in the innermost being, and in the hidden part Thou wilt make me know wisdom. Purify me with hyssop, and I shall be clean; wash me, and I shall be whiter than snow. Make me to hear joy and gladness, let the bones which Thou hast broken rejoice. Hide Thy face from my sins, and blot out all my iniquities. Create in me a clean heart, O God, and renew a steadfast spirit within me. Do not cast me away from Thy presence, and do not take Thy Holy Spirit from me. Restore to me the joy of Thy salvation, and sustain me with a willing spirit. Then I will teach transgressors Thy ways, and sinners will be converted to Thee. Deliver me from bloodguiltiness, O God, Thou God of my salvation; then my tongue will joyfully sing of Thy righteousness. O Lord, open my lips, that my mouth may declare Thy praise. For Thou dost not delight in sacrifice, otherwise I would give it; Thou art not pleased with burnt offering. The sacrifices of God are a broken spirit; a broken and a contrite heart, O God, Thou wilt not despise. By Thy favor do good to Zion; build the walls of Jerusalem. Then Thou wilt

God took away David's sin, but David was left with the memory.

delight in righteous sacrifices, in burnt offering and whole burnt offering; then young bulls will be offered on Thine altar (Psalm 51:1–19).

## GOD DESCRIBES GOD

Soon after receiving the law on Mount Sinai, Moses made an unusual request: "I pray Thee, show me Thy glory!" God said no one can see His face and live, but God agreed to let Moses see Him, with His hand covering Him, as He passed by:

> Then the Lord passed by in front of him and proclaimed, "The Lord, the Lord God, compassionate and gracious, slow to anger, and abounding in lovingkindness and truth; who keeps lovingkindness for thousands, who forgives iniquity, transgression and sin" (Exodus 34:6–7).

Let's analyze these attributes that describe God's nature.

♦ Compassionate—having compassion, having pity, being concerned

♦ Gracious—benevolent, favorable, showing grace

♦ Slow to anger—patient, long-suffering

♦ Abounding in lovingkindness—full of mercy

♦ Abounding in truth—full of honesty and what is real and authentic

♦ Forgives iniquity, transgression, and sin—forgives and forgets all wrongdoings

We are struck with God's honesty. Nothing is "put on" or fake about Him. He is YHWH—"I AM WHO I AM"—the eternal one (Exodus 3:14).

## A WOMAN AFTER GOD'S OWN HEART

David wrote: "For Thou, Lord, art good, and ready to forgive, and abundant in lovingkindness to all who call upon Thee" (Psalm 86:5). God is full of mercy, always ready to forgive those who ask. If we expect to please Him, we must be ready to forgive, too.

David has gone down in history because of God's commendation of him: "a man after my heart" (Acts 13:22). Nothing could be more wonderful than hearing God say, "I have found Becky, daughter of Lea and Russ, to be a woman after My own heart, who will do all My will."

How about you, my friend? Fill in the blanks with your name: "I have found _____, daughter of _____ and _____, to be a woman after my own heart, who will do all my will."

You can make it happen. Remember, God is just sitting on ready—ready to change your life!

## THOUGHTS TO PONDER

1. How should the will of God fit into our lives?

2. What were David's first words to Nathan when he was confronted with his sin with Bathsheba?

3. What are some qualities that made Uriah one of David's best soldiers?

4. Define *ready* (Psalm 86:5). How does repentance define the difference between forgiveness and being "ready to forgive"?

## SONG FOR TODAY

### ABIDE WITH ME

Abide with me; fast falls the even tide;
The darkness deepens: Lord, with me abide!
When other helpers fail, and comforts flee,
Help of the helpless, O abide with me!

Swift to its close ebbs out life's little day;
Earth's joys grow dim, its glories pass away;
Change and decay in all around I see;
O Thou who changest not, abide with me!

I need Thy presence ev'ry passing hour;
What but Thy grace can foil the tempter's pow'r?
Who like Thyself my guide and stay can be?
Thru cloud and sunshine, O abide with me!

Hold Thou Thy cross before my closing eyes;
Shine thru the gloom, and point me to the skies;
Heav'n's morning breaks, and earth's vain shadows flee;
In life, in death, O Lord, abide with me!

## PRAYER FOR TODAY

*Dear Father, we are so grateful for all the blessings You have showered on us today. Lord, we love You and adore Your holy name. How thankful we are that You love us the way You do and bestow such tender mercies upon our heads!*

*O God, You know our hearts and our deepest thoughts. Please change our lives and help us to become better children and better servants to You. Thank You for forgiving our sins and iniquities and allowing us to plead our petitions and prayers before Your throne.*

*Please give us strong bodies and good health so we may have a long time to serve You, if that is Your will, Lord. Have mercy on us, Father, and forgive us. Help us to lift up our eyes and see the harvest before us. In Jesus' name. Amen.*

# BECKY'S MEMORIES

## THE SATAN FACTOR

Do you like to argue? Do you relish the stinging, verbal barbs, the venom spewing or the selfishness exhibited when actions scream, "I want my own way"? Most of us want peace. Oh, not just world peace but peace in our lives, in the church, at home—in all of our relationships.

Here is a much-quoted verse from my childhood: "Do not let the sun go down on your wrath" (Ephesians 4:26 NKJV). That means, fix the problem before you lay your head on your pillow. Sleep does not come easily when one is upset with a family member. Our family discussed disagreements. We heard both sides, and many times offered prayers before peace prevailed. The wrath had to be excised so love and peace could reign again. When God rules our lives, even ugly arguments can be resolved and hugs restored.

There are no words comparable to "I am sorry." I call them magic words. They precede peace and harmony and restore relationships. We need to be able to say "I'm sorry" easily and mean it wholeheartedly. When uttered with penitence, they result in forgiveness and healing on both sides.

A snowy winter day in New England was the setting for an infamous feud between my parents. Dad had bought two, very used, snowmobiles, and he and Mom enjoyed snowmobiling. They were a sight, flying through the snow until one of them fell off. Usually Mom was the first casualty. Dad then pulled the heavy "skimadoo," as Mom called it, out of the snowbank and she hopped on again.

One particular icy day, Mom and Dad planned a venture through the woods. Mom set off but soon noticed Dad was not behind her. She continued, assuming he would catch up. After traveling quite a distance, Mom's snowmobile lurched into a snowbank. Climbing off, she turned, expecting to see Dad coming to her rescue. But there was no Dad. She tried to drag the snowmobile back on track, but it was too heavy and cumbersome. Mom's only solution was to walk back, hoping with every step that Dad would be just around the next corner.

Have you ever walked a long way in heavy snow while bundled to the max? Mom looked like a cross between the Abominable Snowman and the Pillsbury Dough Boy. She trudged all the way back home, devising all kinds of agonizing torture for her beloved.

Just as Mom walked into the yard, Dad appeared around the corner of the house. Mom looked him squarely in the eye and stated slowly and in staccato fashion: "There is nothing you can say!"

Dad softly said, "Lea, I am sorry. My snowmobile was out of gas." The air went right out of that Pillsbury Dough Boy.

I tell you this family secret because I want you to know that everyone argues. There is no perfect marriage or perfect relationship. Many new Christians mistakenly presume that Christians never experience any struggles, that all Christians love each other, and that there is never any conflict in the church. Nothing is further from the truth.

Problems in the Christian's life will arise because of one constant force: the Satan factor. Satan thrives on conflict. One of his goals is to make our lives miserable. He loves to cause division and arguments among brothers—and sisters!

We often forget the force behind rampant jealousy, envy, negativism, and cattiness. Satan! Some folks are singing "oh, how I love Jesus" one moment and verbally stabbing a sister as soon as the closing prayer is over.

I know how important friendships are for a woman—I am one. We need women in our lives—kindred spirits that offer support, encouragement, laughter, and tears. Christian women certainly know how to assist and pray for a sister in any crisis, illness, or problem.

Friendships require sacrifice, money, and time. We women are willing to go the distance, not only because we have an innate need to nurture others, but also because we need our girlfriends. However, don't forget that Satan knows us; he is lurking, constantly planning more attacks on us. The last thing he wants is for any of us to befriend our sisters.

Take note: As a Christian woman, you will experience a close friendship that suddenly falls apart. Your bosom buddy will become a mortal enemy. Whether the estrangement occurs because of a misunderstanding, argument, or a huge faux pas, the friendship will be irrevocably broken, never to be repaired. Neither of you wants this to happen or even imagines that it could happen, but it will happen because Satan walks to and fro upon this earth, seeking a relationship to devour. You will experience the deepest woe and pain because a sister is no longer that—a sister to you. She is your adversary now. And your heart is broken, absolutely broken. To make matters worse, you cannot talk with her anymore.

This is no small matter. We have entrusted, given, and sacrificed on that altar called friendship, and it has been irreparably torn down. Our husbands offer all the help they can, but it is God who will solve this problem. We pour out our hearts to Him at the Begging Place, and He listens and comforts and soothes our anguished souls.

Yes, this happened to me. What did I do? I took up permanent residence at the Begging Place. All I did was pray. I went to bed, heartbroken and praying; I woke up, heartbroken and praying. It was difficult to worship because I was so absorbed in the crisis. But the Father knew what I was feeling. Time passed, and at the right time, God sent other women into my life. Time healed the wound.

The world demands closure. But we don't always receive closure when a friendship sours. Christians must learn patience, which literally means "long-suffering" or "bearing up under." God suffers long with us, and we must suffer long with others. We must keep on keeping on. Stay the course. Don't look back.

You loved that friend. But that relationship changed. What if you both attend the same congregation? How difficult! You must still love each other's souls, although things have changed. The Father will deliver you from painful situations because He knows all.

You see, the Begging Place is our classroom. Here we learn to surrender, and here we are the most vulnerable, because we open our hearts to the Godhead. At the Begging Place, the Trinity begins its respective work for us. The Spirit comforts our souls and the Master Teacher helps us to become what we should be for God. The Father picks us up and sets us on our course with Him again. How magnificent they are!

If we really want to please God, we will study His Word and pray every day. When we study the Bible, we learn how to use this sword of the Spirit to cut out all the bad in us. That same sword replaces the voids in our hearts with the fruit of the Spirit: love, joy, peace, patience, kindness, goodness, faithfulness, gentleness, and self-control (Galatians 5:22–23).

Pleasing the Father demands that we learn to say "I'm sorry" and "please forgive me." Pleasing our Father also requires us to make peace with our families before we sleep.

You've heard, "It is better to have loved and lost than never to have loved at all." True. And so is this statement: "Friendship is from God." Friendships are necessary for healthy Christian living. He knows we need each other. Let us beg Him to help us become the woman He wants us to become. Let us hear Him softly whisper: "Remember, My daughter, a friend loves at all times."

Dear Friend,

I just had to send a note to tell you how much I love you and care about you. I saw you yesterday walking with your friends. I waited all day hoping you would want to talk with Me also. As evening drew near, I gave you a sunset to close your day and a cool breeze to rest you. And I waited. But you never came. It hurt Me, but I still love you because I am your friend.

I saw you fall asleep last night and I longed to touch your brow. So I spilled moonlight on your pillow and your face. Again I waited, wanting to rush down so we could talk. I have so many gifts for you. But you awakened late the next day and rushed off to work. My tears were in the rain.

Today you looked sad, so all alone. It makes My heart ache because I understand. My friends often let Me down and hurt Me, too. But I love you. Oh, if you would only listen to Me. I really love you. I try to tell you in the blue sky and in the quiet green grass. I whisper it in the leaves on the trees and breathe it in the colors of the flowers. I shout it to you in the mountain streams and give the birds love songs to sing. I clothe you with warm sunshine and perfume the air with nature's scents. My love for you is deeper than the oceans and bigger than your biggest want or need.

If you only knew how much I want to help you. I want you to meet My Son. He wants to help you, too. My Son is that way, you know. Just call Me, ask Me, talk with Me. Please, please don't forget Me. I have so much to share with you. But I won't hassle you any further. You are free to call Me anytime. It's up to you. I'll wait because I love you!

Your Friend,

God

CHAPTER 12

# THE LORD ANSWERS ALL PRAYERS

My soul waits in silence for God only;
from Him is my salvation. He only is my rock
and my salvation, my stronghold;
I shall not be greatly shaken . . .
Trust in Him at all times; O people;
pour out your heart before Him;
God is a refuge for us
(Psalm 62:1-8).

Is anything bothering you today? Christians can pray to God about anything on their hearts. "Let us therefore draw near with confidence to the throne of grace, that we may receive mercy and may find grace to help in time of need" (Hebrews 4:16). What comfort!

God answers our prayers in three ways: "Yes," "No," and "Wait awhile." We know that God is aware of our requests, but His time frame is not always in sync with ours. Here is a psalm that has helped me to cope with huge and life-altering changes:

> My soul waits in silence for God only; from Him is my salvation. He only is my rock and my salvation, my stronghold; I shall not be greatly shaken . . . My soul, wait in silence for God only, for my hope is from Him. He only is my rock and my salvation, my stronghold; I shall not be shaken. On God my salvation and my glory rest; the rock of my strength, my refuge is in God. Trust in Him at all times, O people; pour out your heart before Him; God is a refuge for us (Psalm 62:1–8).

Learning to wait on God is important for us all. But have we learned to "wait in silence for God"? We are an impatient society. We are used to life in the fast lane, express checkouts, and no waiting lines. And if we don't get our way, buddy, watch out! However, God makes us slow down and realize He will work things out at precisely the right time. Learning to wait is a faith-building exercise. Through waiting, God teaches us patience, endurance, and persistence. David says, "I shall not be greatly shaken." That's similar to the song we sang when I was a little girl: "I Shall Not Be Moved."

## THE ANSWER IS NO!

Sometimes God says no, and it stays no! We do not always understand why; we may even experience anxiety and exasperation. But the answer is still no and will never be anything else. That is hard for us to accept. We detest being told no, because we want our own way!

### THE SERENITY PRAYER

God grant me the serenity
To accept the things I cannot change,
Courage to change the things I can,
And wisdom to know the difference.

One of my mother's famous sayings was, "Accept the things you cannot change." I didn't want to accept them; I wanted to change them. But many situations have to be accepted because they are not going to change. Lying on the floor kicking and screaming serves only to get us dirty, tired, and hoarse! No matter how angry or upset we get, and no matter how much we beg God, some matters will never be altered—period! God has spoken.

> Satan is around every corner, and life is not fair. It takes only a second to fall.

### REMOVE THE THORN? NO!

The apostle Paul was familiar with this philosophy of "accepting the things you cannot change." How often Christians hear sermons about Paul's thorn in the flesh! There are numerous speculations and conjectures as to exactly what that thorn was, but the reality of it is, God never granted Paul's request to remove it:

And because of the surpassing greatness of the revelations, for this reason, to keep me from exalting myself, there was given me a thorn in the flesh, a messenger of Satan to buffet me—to keep me from exalting myself! Concerning this I entreated the Lord three times that it might depart from me. And He has said to me, "My grace is sufficient for you, for power is perfected in weakness." . . . Therefore I am well content with weaknesses, with insults, with distresses, with persecutions, with difficulties, for Christ's sake; for when I am weak; then I am strong (2 Corinthians 12:7–10).

What does "when I am weak; then I am strong" mean? Paul meant that when he experienced the frailties of the flesh and persecution as a Christian, he had to depend on God's deliverance and strength. Paul knew his walk with God depended on a good and constant prayer life. When his flesh was weak, he could still be strong because all he had to do was ask. On his knees Paul experienced a closeness to his Father that only a son realizes. Someone has wisely said, "When we are sad, we are closer to God."

## WORRY? NO!

"Pray without ceasing" (1 Thessalonians 5:17). Don't stop praying. Why? Because Satan is around every corner, and life is not fair. It takes only a second to fall.

In Jesus' *Sermon on the Mount*, the Savior commands us:

Do not be anxious then, saying, "What shall we eat?" or "What shall we drink?" or "With what shall we clothe ourselves?" For all these things the Gentiles eagerly seek; for your heavenly Father knows that you need these things. But seek first His kingdom and His righteousness; and all these things shall be added to you. Therefore do not be anxious for tomorrow; for tomorrow will care for itself. Each day has enough trouble of its own (Matthew 6:31–34).

We need the presence of the Father, the Son, and the Holy Spirit every moment. Worrying about clothes, shelter, and food will accomplish nothing but gray hair, ulcers, and wrinkles. God knows what we need. He has it all handled.

Our job is to seek God. We must live like Him, talk to Him, obey His will, and accept the "Yes," the "No," and the "Wait awhile."

## SAVE THE CHILD? NO!

God told David no when he begged for his child's life. God said no to the great apostle Paul. God told Hannah to wait awhile when she prayed for a child. When God's own Son begged Him to let the cup of the crucifixion pass from Him, God said no.

Learning to accept the things we cannot change is often painful, but it can make us grow if we let it. Our Father knows what is best for Him and us. In this process of growing up, we become more like Him and His wonderful Son. People will start to see the resemblance.

Some Bible passages are absolute "zingers." They scream for us to stop and listen to God. Psalm 46:10 is one of those zingers. This psalm offered peace and hope to the people of God, and it continues to calm many a troubled soul today: "Cease striving and know that I am God." Here's another translation: "Be still, and know that I am God" (NKJV).

> Stop fretting, stop worrying, stop agonizing, stop trying to make something work out. Stop!

In our hurried, stressful, and busy lives, this psalm stops us dead in our tracks. Stop what? Stop fretting, stop worrying, stop agonizing, stop trying to make something work out. Stop! Literally, God is saying, "Let go!" Let go of what? Of whatever is wringing out our minds and hearts.

"Know that I am God." Who can read this and not feel God's strength, power, and peace? God is in control and His will shall be done. Of that we can rest assured. Offer the prayer, let God answer it His way, and accept it whatever it is.

## MERCY AND GRACE

The theme of Hebrews is *better*. A better law, a better covenant, and a better high priest. The old law died and was nailed to the cross with Jesus (Colossians 2:14). No longer did animals have to be sacrificed for sin, and no longer did a human high priest act as an intercessor between God and man. Christ changed all that:

> Since then we have a great high priest who has passed through the heavens, Jesus the Son of God, let us hold fast our confession. For we do not have a high priest who cannot sympathize with our weaknesses, but One who has been tempted in all things as we are, yet without sin. Let us therefore draw near with confidence to the throne of grace, that we may receive mercy and may find grace to help in time of need (Hebrews 4:14–16).

The high priest of the old law was a man who sinned. Jesus was tempted in all things and yet did not sin. When He died and rose again, He became our high priest and ushered in the new law. He can understand what we are going through and intercede for us! We Christians are most blessed to have the very Son of God pleading our cause before God.

Jesus knows what it is like to be lonely. He has felt the pain of losing someone you love. He understands what a family can experience—all its problems and emotions—because He once was part of an earthly family. Verse 15 describes Jesus as the high priest who intercedes for us. Verses 14–16 offer hope, promise, and comfort. It is not that we will someday receive mercy and grace, but that we can draw near to God boldly so that we may receive them now. Mercy and grace are possible. Think about it for a moment—mercy and grace. This passage does not say we will receive justice, but mercy and grace when we approach our God in prayer. I am glad Jesus intercedes for me.

The New King James Version uses the word "boldly" instead of "with confidence." We can walk into God's throne room and confidently approach Him. We will receive mercy at His throne of grace. And isn't that what we really desire and need? How do you feel about this Scripture in Hebrews? Does it touch your heart? Has it changed your prayer life?

## I OFTEN SAY MY PRAYERS

I often say my prayers,
But do I ever pray?
And do the wishes of my heart
Go with the words I say?

I may as well kneel down
And worship gods of stone,
As offer to the living God
A prayer of words alone.

For words without the heart,
The Lord will never hear,
Nor will He to those lips attend
Whose prayers are not sincere.

Lord, teach me what I need,
And teach me how to pray;
Nor let me ask Thy grace,
Not feeling what I say.

—Author Unknown

## THREE IMPORTANT QUESTIONS

Several things happen as we pour out our hearts before His throne. What should our attitude be toward God? How should we feel about our sins? Where do I stand before Him?

- *Do I have the right attitude?* We can approach our God with confidence but never with arrogance. Haughtiness has no part in a Christian's life, especially when addressing God. Humility is a must. Notice the first of seven things God hates:

> There are six things which the Lord hates, yes, seven which are an abomination to Him: haughty eyes, a lying tongue, and hands that shed innocent blood, a heart that devises wicked plans, feet that run rapidly to evil, a false witness who utters lies, and one who spreads strife among brothers (Proverbs 6:16–19).

In Jesus' parable of the two men who went up to pray in the temple, the publican came away justified. The Pharisee was too proud to be forgiven (Luke 18:10–14).

✠ *Do I have a penitent heart?* We cannot approach God's marvelous throne of grace so confidently that we forget how sinful we really are. We must humbly lay our sins at the Master's feet before He will hear us.

> Acknowledge the evil of sin; ask God to make you feel it. Do not treat it as a trifle, for it is none. To redeem the sinner from the effects of sin, Christ Himself had to die; and unless you are delivered from it, you must die eternally. Therefore, do not play with sin. Do not confess it as though it were some trivial fault that would not have been noticed unless God had been too severe; but labor to see sin as God sees it, as an offense against all that is good, a rebellion against all that is kind. See it to be treason, to be ingratitude, to be a low and base thing. Never expect that the King of heaven will pardon a traitor if he will not confess and forsake his treason. Even the tenderest father expects the child to humble himself when he has offended, and he will not withdraw his frown from him until with tears the child has said, "Father, I have sinned" (Spurgeon, *The Power in Prayer*, 90).

Those last three words are the same ones the prodigal son said to his father when he returned home. He continued: "I am no longer worthy to be called your son" (Luke 15:21). In his quest for the "good life" of wine, women, and song, the young man had learned many great lessons. Penniless and living with the hogs, he was truly sorry for all the worry, sorrow, and troubles he had brought upon his father. We, too, must be sorry for our own sins. When we return home with a contrite spirit, our Father rushes to meet us and forgive us.

> Haughtiness has no part in a Christian's life, especially when addressing God.

◆ Humble yourselves, therefore, under the mighty hand of God, that He may exalt you at the proper time, casting all your anxiety upon Him, because He cares for you (1 Peter 5:6–7).

◆ "For my hand made all these things, thus all these things came into being," declares the Lord. "But to this one I will look, to Him who is humble and contrite of spirit, and who trembles at my word" (Isaiah 66:2).

◆ The sacrifices of God are a broken spirit; a broken and a contrite heart, O God, Thou wilt not despise (Psalm 51:17).

✴ *Where do I stand?* Proceed confidently into the throne room of God. Stand before the Lord Almighty—Yahweh, El Adonai, El Shaddai, El Elohim. He is the mighty God, and we are the sinful humans. He is the Creator of the universe, and we are dust and children of wrath. We must be sorry for our sins and acknowledge Him for who He is. David said it this way:

> Come, let us worship and bow down; let us kneel before the Lord our Maker. For He is our God, and we are the people of His pasture, and the sheep of His hand (Psalm 95:6–7).

God's throne is one of grace, a place where undeserving sinners can go. God's throne is a place where hope abides, where love abides, and where mercy and grace flow freely. Mercy is lovingkindness, and grace is unmerited favor. What wonderful qualities God extends as He listens to our awkward prayers. How kind He is to us! The Scripture rings true: "Every good thing bestowed and every perfect gift is from above, coming down from the Father of lights, with whom there is no variation, or shifting shadow" (James 1:17).

> God has all the answers for every problem, every crisis—anytime, anywhere.

As we seek His face and make our supplications before Him, may we never forget that we are in the throne room of Almighty God. He chooses whether or not to let us in. Surrendering everything to God is a humbling experience. We are sometimes so concerned about our needs that we do not comprehend the enormity of the situation. We are in the presence of God, our Sovereign and heavenly Father. This is serious business!

Isaiah, the messianic prophet, summarizes this concept: "But we are all like an unclean thing, and all our righteousnesses are like filthy rags" (Isaiah 64:6 NKJV).

# FORGET NONE OF HIS BENEFITS

Let's be honest here. We know what we are. Even if we were to perform great accomplishments for God until the end of time, we could never earn the sweet gifts of prayer, forgiveness, and salvation. Only by His marvelous and wonderful grace are we able to approach His throne and pour out our hearts before Him.

Let's look at this thought-provoking passage one more time: "Let us therefore draw near with confidence to the throne of grace, that we may receive mercy and may find grace to help in time of need" (Hebrews 4:16). My favorite part of this verse is "to help in time of need." This passage is about seeking God when our lives are in a crisis, but I always need His help. I struggle daily with character flaws. Like Paul, I find myself doing the things I should not do and not doing the things I should do (Romans 7:19). There is a place where a Christian can find help, and not just any help but His help. The Christian is never left alone in the dark to wonder what the next step should be, for God has all the answers for every problem, every crisis—anytime, anywhere. Listen to these beautiful words:

> Bless the Lord, O my soul, and forget none of His benefits; who pardons all your iniquities, who heals all your diseases; who redeems your life from the pit; who crowns you with lovingkindness and compassion; who satisfies your years with good things, so that your youth is renewed like the eagle (Psalm 103:2–5).

> For Thou, Lord, art good, and ready to forgive, and abundant in lovingkindness to all who call upon Thee (Psalm 86:5).

I have gone to the Begging Place in sheer despair, able only to say, "Lord, please help me. Please help." And my Helper was there. I was shown mercy, and I was given grace. You see, the Begging Place is the mercy seat of God! Oh, my friend, God can handle it all; it's not too much for Him.

## THOUGHTS TO PONDER

1. What does Hebrews 4:16 tell us about prayer?

2. Why is it hard for us to wait on God?

3. Does God always answer our prayers the way we want Him to answer them?

4. Why is it important that Jesus intercede for us?

## SONG FOR TODAY

### IF I HAVE WOUNDED ANY SOUL

If I have wounded any soul today,
If I have caused one foot to go astray,
If I have walked in my own willful way,
Dear Lord, forgive.

If I have been perverse or hard or cold,
If I have longed for shelter in Thy fold,
When Thou hast given me some fort to hold,
Dear Lord, forgive.

Forgive the sins I have confessed to Thee;
Forgive the secret sins I do not see;
O guide me, love me, and my keeper be,
In Jesus' name. Amen.

## PRAYER FOR TODAY

*Our dear Father, we bow before You and acknowledge that You are our Maker and the Supreme Creator of the universe. Thank You for creating us and loving us and giving us salvation through Your Son, Jesus. Please forgive us when we fail You, O Lord. Thank You for the privilege of talking to You and telling You what is on our hearts and minds. Lord, thank You for answering our prayers the way You do. Help us to have patience when we do not understand Your answers, and help us always to say, "Your will be done in all things."*

*Walk with us, O God, and may we not displease You in our worship and in our lives we offer as living sacrifices. You are our omniscient, omnipresent, and omnipotent Father, and we stand in awe of You. In Jesus' name. Amen.*

# BECKY'S MEMORIES

## THE OLD RUGGED CROSS

Do you have a favorite spiritual song, one that touches your heart? It is amazing how some hymns hold such powerful meanings. A special memory comes to me every time I sing "The Old Rugged Cross."

It was a Sunday morning. The four of us and our guest were seated on our regular pew. Our two children were elated because "Ticky"—their pet name for my mother—was visiting. We sang "The Old Rugged Cross" to help prepare our minds for the Lord's supper. As the haunting melody and stirring lyrics of this beautiful old song fell from our lips, our minds centered on Jesus' sacrifice. Even though this hymn was not on my list of personal favorites, I always loved the sentiments.

Out of the corner of my eye, I noticed my mother was crying. Mom was always emotional; I just thought that the scenes of the cross and its significance were responsible for her falling tears. After we arrived home, she told me the following experience which added an extra dimension to her personal faith:

> I was a young mother of a seven year old, a four year old, and a new baby. You were that baby, Becky! Because of previous miscarriages, I had begged God for your safe arrival. I had to be especially careful during my pregnancy. Your dad and I began to miss worship occasionally because it was such a strain with the little ones. We used my pregnancy as an excuse to drift away from God. We both knew better, but we allowed Satan to influence our faithfulness.
>
> When you were born, Becky, I had a C-section. That was highly unusual "way back then." In addition, my doctor decided to perform a hysterectomy immediately after your birth. This was a double whammy when it came to recuperation. I was also experiencing a personal fear of death. My mother had died at almost the same age I was then. I worried constantly that I would leave three motherless children.
>
> Finally, the Sunday morning arrived when I was strong enough for all of us to worship together. Now we were a family of five, sitting on our favorite pew. When time came for the Lord's supper,

we sang "The Old Rugged Cross." As I sat holding you in my arms and singing that hymn, I rededicated my life to my Father.

I promised to be faithful to Him always, no matter what. I promised to be a strong Christian wife and mother. I promised to raise my children in the Lord and do His will. I sorrowfully remembered the huge price Jesus paid for me, personally. And with tears rolling down my cheeks, I sang "The Old Rugged Cross" in a way that I had never sung before—with a little baby girl in my arms.

On a hill far away stood an old rugged cross,
The emblem of suff'ring and shame;
And I love that old cross where the dearest and best
For a world of lost sinners was slain.

O that old rugged cross, so despised by the world,
Has a wondrous attraction for me;
For the dear Lamb of God left His glory above,
To bear it to dark Calvary.

In that old rugged cross, stained with blood so divine,
A wondrous beauty I see;
For 'twas on that old cross Jesus suffered and died,
To pardon and sanctify me.

To that old rugged cross I will ever be true,
Its shame and reproach gladly bear;
Then He'll call me some day to my home far away,
Where His glory forever I'll share.

Chorus: So I'll cherish the old rugged cross,
Till my trophies at last I lay down;
I will cling to the old rugged cross,
And exchange it some day for a crown.

At the end of her story, Mother added, "So you can imagine how it was for me today when we worshiped together and sang once again, 'The Old Rugged Cross.' Here I am—some thirty years later—sitting on a pew beside that little girl with her own children. And we are all together, faithful to the Lord. I have kept my promise, and I will always be faithful to it and to God. And here is that little baby girl, all grown up with her own children and faithful to the Lord. Oh, how good God is to me!"

I understand now what she felt. After I had a family, Mom often said, "You just don't know what comfort it is to know that on Sundays, as your daddy and I worship the Lord, all my children are worshiping the Lord, too!" Now I know what she was talking about.

To this day, there is nothing sweeter than knowing my children are in the assembly as I am, even though miles may separate us.

"The Old Rugged Cross" is probably the sweetest song ever written. I love it now! Not only did my mother sing it, she lived it. And as I sing it—usually with tears—I remember the cross my Savior died upon. But I also remember a young mother who began her walk with God all over again.

BECKY, MOM, AND JENNIFER

CHAPTER 13

# JESUS, THE FIGURE IN THE SHADOWS

*In the days of His flesh, He offered up both prayers and*
*supplications with loud crying and tears to the*
*One able to save Him from death, and He was heard*
*because of His piety. Although He was a Son,*
*He learned obedience from the things which He suffered.*
*And having been made perfect, He became to all those*
*who obey Him the source of eternal salvation*
*(Hebrews 5:7-9).*

The following stanzas of the hymn, "When My Love for Christ Grows Weak," are a beautiful depiction of the Begging Place, a quiet evening scene in Gethsemane. That suffering, friendless one weeping and praying is our Savior. The Messiah's earthly mission is coming to an end. Jesus knows that the ordeal of the cross is before Him. His final chapter of living here as a human is drawing to a close.

> When my love to Christ grows weak,
> When for deeper faith I seek,
> Then in tho't I go to thee,
> Garden of Gethsemane!
>
> There I walk amid the shades,
> While the ling'ring twilight fades,
> See that suff'ring, friendless One,
> Weeping, praying there alone.

At the Begging Place we see Jesus as both God and man. His human side was begging. Some other cup perhaps, but not the cup of the cross. How many times had Jesus passed Calvary and seen victims hanging on the crosses? How often had He thought to Himself, "Someday this will surely be Me"?

Jesus the Son was God in the flesh. He knew the cross had to be experienced; He must die. That had always been the plan. The cross would be the biggest test of His life. He would endure the beating, the mocking, and the death on the cross because He knew that would not be the end of the story. He also was sure His Father would be by His side.

## FOR THE JOY SET BEFORE HIM

Jesus Christ came to die and to rise again. He was willing to take on the sins of the world—past, present, and future, even your sins and mine, in order that we could live eternally with Him. Paul said, "He made Him who knew no sin to be sin on our behalf, that we might become the righteousness of God in Him" (2 Corinthians 5:21).

> *Why would any church need to be reminded of what Jesus gave up for them?*

The cross was joy for Jesus! How can that be? How could something so painful and shameful bring happiness? Listen to what the Bible says: "Fixing our eyes on Jesus, the author and perfecter of faith, who for the joy set before Him endured the cross, despising the shame, and has sat down at the right hand of the throne of God" (Hebrews 12:2). Yes, Jesus hated the shame of the cross, but He endured the suffering with joy. And God honored His Son by seating Him on His right side.

"The joy that was set before him" was the joy of reversing, at last, the tragic defeat of humanity in the Paradise of Eden; the joy of knowing that Satan's purpose of destroying man was foiled; the joy of "bringing many sons unto glory" (Hebrews 2:10); the joy of the saved entering heaven "with songs and everlasting joy upon their heads" (Isaiah 35:10); the joy of the herald angels' "tidings of great joy which shall be to all people" (Luke 2:10); and such marvelous joy that, in truth, no vocabulary may describe it, no rhetoric suggest it, or finite mind fully conceive of it (James Burton Coffman, *Hebrews* [A.C.U. Press: Abilene, TX, 1971], 289).

## HAVE THIS ATTITUDE

While we are at the cross, let's look at one more beautiful passage in the Bible:

> Have this attitude in yourselves which was also in Christ Jesus, who, although He existed in the form of God, did not regard equality with God a thing to be grasped, but emptied Himself, taking the form of a bond-servant, and being made in the likeness of men. And being found in appearance as a man, He humbled Himself by becoming obedient to the point of death, even death on a cross (Philippians 2:5–9).

Why would any church need to be reminded of what Jesus gave up for them? The church is made up of people, people who have character flaws, people who are jealous of others. When personality conflicts arise, it is easy to forget that our primary focus is Christ and His love. The church at Philippi was embroiled in such a struggle when Paul wrote the above Scripture to set matters aright. When Christians are willing to have the mind of Christ—a willingness to do anything the Father asks—God will exalt them.

## OBEDIENCE THROUGH SUFFERING

The writer of Hebrews wrote about Jesus' last days on earth, His prayers at the Begging Place, and His sufferings:

> In the days of His flesh, He offered up both prayers and supplications with loud crying and tears to the One able to save Him from death, and He was heard because of His piety. Although he was a Son, He learned obedience from the things which He suffered. And having been made perfect, He became to all those who obey Him the source of eternal salvation (Hebrews 5:7–9).

Although Jesus had no sin, He still suffered in spite of His perfect obedience. That obedience caused bitter hatred against Him and provided the occasion for every blow that fell upon His person. Christ was hated in the same way Abel was hated. You know why Cain killed him: "And wherefore slew he him? Because his own works were evil, and his brother's righteous" (1 John 3:12 KJV).

## No Other Way

They didn't really have to force Him
To the cross, He'd gladly go,
There was no other way to save us,
From the sins we've done below.
There was no other way to meet Him
In the everlasting land,
No other way to be forgiven
Than in the washing of the Lamb.

—Lea Fowler

As the children of God, we learn obedience by suffering. God's way will always be the best way, even when it hurts. God never promised anyone a pain-free life. There will be many times of extreme stress, deep pain, and true sufferings in our lives. There will also be many moments of great joy. However, when we are suffering, we are becoming like Christ. Let us never forget that.

Beloved, do not be surprised at the fiery ordeal among you, which comes upon you for your testing, as though some strange thing were happening to you; but to the degree that you share the sufferings of Christ, keep on rejoicing; so that also at the revelation of His glory, you may rejoice with exultation. If you are reviled for the name of Christ, you are blessed, because the Spirit of glory and of God rests upon you (1 Peter 4:12–14).

Blessed be the God and Father of our Lord Jesus Christ, the Father of mercies and God of all comfort; who comforts us in all our affliction so that we may be able to comfort those who are in any affliction with the comfort with which we ourselves are comforted by God. For just as the sufferings of Christ are ours in abundance, so also our comfort is abundant through Christ (2 Corinthians 1:3–5).

## Satan in the Church

We are proud to wear Christ's name because we are on our way to heaven. He said, "I am the way, and the truth, and the life; no one comes to the Father, but through Me" (John 14:6). Our Jesus leads the way home; He *is* the way home.

We gather on the first day of the week to praise God in song, in teaching, in giving, in reading the Bible, in praying, and in partaking of the Lord's supper. These are the acts of our worship to our Father, and He has commanded us to observe them. We take these acts seriously, because we take our worship of the Godhead seriously. Above all things, we must please our Father in our worship.

The Bible cautions us to prepare ourselves to worship God. Solomon was inspired to write: "Guard your steps as you go to the house of God, and draw near to listen rather than to offer the sacrifice of fools; for they do not know they are doing evil" (Ecclesiastes 5:1).

How do we guard our steps? By controlling our thoughts and focusing our minds on worship. We are coming into the presence of God the Father, God the Son, and God the Holy Spirit. This is serious business! How difficult it is to fly into the church's parking lot with the radio blaring rock music one minute and be mentally ready to meet the Lord the next minute!

> "Guard your steps as you go to the house of God, and draw near to listen rather than to offer the sacrifice of fools."

We should avoid foolish and flippant words as we gather to worship. How many times has someone hurt our feelings as we entered the Lord's house for worship? Or have we hurt someone else as she was preparing for worship? We forget Satan comes to worship. He is smart. He already has the world in his pocket, and he knows where to find us!

Notice that God tells us to draw near to listen and not to give our opinion! We should let the teacher share what he or she has prepared. Some feel they must express an opinion on every little thing. They usually do not know that their inconsiderate participation creates misery for the class. (Haven't you ever wished that that "someone" would just shut up?)

Likewise, in order to worship properly, we must learn the art of being quiet and still. Observe the last sentence in Ecclesiastes 5:1. We can offer the sacrifice of fools and not know that we are doing wrong or evil.

## CHRIST'S FUNERAL

When we pause for the memorial feast of our Savior, we are at Christ's funeral. We remember His death. With our finite minds and feeble brains, every Sunday we picture His scourging, His crucifixion, and His resurrection. It never becomes mundane unless we allow it to do so. The feast is designed to draw us to the cross and His sacrifice. We are not remembering His great sacrifice alone, but we are also communing with our brethren across the face of this earth.

When we meet in sweet communion
Where the feast divine is spread;
Hearts are brought in closer union
While partaking of the bread.

Precious feast all else surpassing,
Wondrous love for you and me,
While we feast Christ gently whispers:
"Do this in My memory."

Concentrating during the Lord's supper is not easy. Crying babies, people whispering, or someone's stomach growling draws our minds from the cross. Satan tries hard to keep us from focusing on the most sacred gift. Proper worship requires a lot of mental discipline and practice.

One way to keep your mind on the Lord's supper is to read songs about Jesus' death. Our hymnals are full of precious, sweet, and purposeful hymns that will help you: "The Old Rugged Cross," "Beneath the Cross of Jesus," "When We Meet in Sweet Communion," and "I Gave My Live for Thee." My two favorites are "When My Love for Christ Grows Weak" and "When I Survey the Wondrous Cross." As the bread is passed and the fruit of the vine is served, I often read these songs.

> Proper worship requires a lot of mental discipline and practice.

I picture myself walking through the Garden of Gethsemane and seeing Jesus as He prays in the shadows that Thursday evening. I watch as He cries and prays to His Father. My heart is touched as I imagine His blood, sweat, and tears while He is praying, prostrate on the ground. I look over in the distance and see His friends asleep, totally unaware of the impending danger. I hear His frequent and urgent cry: "My Father, if it is possible, let this cup pass from Me; yet not as I will, but as Thou wilt" (Matthew 26:39).

All four Gospel accounts describe the heavy sadness of Jesus' prayers in the garden. Jesus even describes how He feels by saying, "My soul is deeply grieved to the point of death" (Mark 14:34).

Mark's account adds that Christ addressed the Father saying, "Abba! Father! All things are possible for Thee; remove this cup from Me; yet not what I will, but what Thou wilt" (Mark 14:36).

Luke, a physician, made two important observations: an angel from heaven came and strengthened Jesus, and Jesus' extreme agony resulted in His sweat being as great drops of blood, a condition known as hematidrosis that sometimes occurs when one experiences profound anguish and stress.

> Night with ebon pinion,
> Brooded o'er the vale;
> All around was silent,
> Save the night-wind's wail,
> When Christ, the Man of Sorrows,
> In tears and sweat and blood,
> Prostrate in the garden,
> Raised His voice to God.

> "Abba, Father, Father,
> If indeed it may,
> Let this cup of anguish
> Pass from Me, I pray;
> Yet, if it must be suffered,
> By Me, Thine only Son,
> Abba, Father, Father,
> Let Thy will be done."

Jesus went to the Begging Place for you and me. He lay on the ground and begged and cried with unusual tears, beseeching His Father for another way. His best friends did not even pray along with Him but fell asleep from exhaustion and sorrow. But Jesus knew the cross was a reality and that God's way was still the best. As we read the accounts in Matthew, Mark, Luke, and John, we can feel Jesus' sorrow, His grief, His sadness, and His indescribable pain.

## YOU ARE THERE

As a little girl, I remember watching my mother partake of the Lord's supper. Silent tears often fell down her face as she prayed. I used to ask myself, "Will I ever cry when I remember what Jesus has done for me?" I know now that when little girls grow up to be dedicated Christians, they cry, too.

Jesus' emotions in the garden and at the cross are real for us. Our hearts are touched, and we weep as we remember our sins and the price Jesus paid for them. Our hearts are filled with love and joy as we recognize that we, too, are children of God and have the right to address the Father in the same way that Christ His Son did. "For you have not received a spirit of slavery leading to fear again, but you have received a spirit of adoption as sons by which we cry out, 'Abba! Father!'" (Romans 8:15).

*Even if I were the only one in this world, Christ would still willingly hang on that cross and die for me.*

My mother and father, as they told of their trips to the Holy Lands, often described an evening devotional in the Garden of Gethsemane. Mother said that after that experience she never could take the Lord's supper the same way as before. She had changed and her prayer life had changed.

> When my love for man grows weak,
> When for stronger faith I seek,
> Hill of Calvary! I go
> To thy scenes of fear and woe.
>
> There behold His agony,
> Suffered on the bitter tree;
> See His anguish, see His faith—
> Love triumphant still in death.

In my mind I go to Calvary. I stand at the cross and pretend that no one exists in the whole, wide world but Jesus Christ and me. We are all alone; it is dark. I know He loves me with a precious and mighty love that I cannot fathom. And I know that even if I really were the only one in this world, Christ would still willingly hang on that cross and die for me. I still cannot fathom this. I never will.

There was One who was willing to die in my stead,
That a soul so unworthy might live;
And the path to the cross He was willing to tread,
All the sins of my life to forgive.
They are nailed to the cross!

They are nailed to the cross!
O how much He was willing to bear!
With what anguish and loss,
Jesus went to the cross!
But He carried my sins with Him there.

Because of His cross, you and I have hope. Because of an empty tomb, you and I have salvation. And because of the Begging Place, you and I can also say, "Abba! Father!"

## THOUGHTS TO PONDER

1. How can we identify with Jesus in the Garden of Gethsemane?

2. Why is it imperative that Christians remember Christ's obedience to God?

3. List the ways Satan can cause conflict as we gather for worship.

4. List the ways we can improve our concentration on the Lord's supper.

## SONG FOR TODAY

## BENEATH THE CROSS OF JESUS

Beneath the cross of Jesus
I fain would take my stand,
The shadow of a mighty rock
Within a weary land,
A home within the wilderness,
A rest upon the way,
From the burning of the noontide heat,
And the burden of the day.

Upon that cross of Jesus,
Mine eye at times can see
The very dying form of One
Who suffered there for me;
And from my smitten heart, with tears
Two wonders I confess:
The wonders of His glorious love,
And my own worthlessness.

I take, O cross, thy shadow
For my abiding place;
I ask no other sunshine than
The sunshine of His face;
Content to let the world go by,
To know no gain nor loss,
My sinful self my only shame,
My glory all the cross!

## PRAYER FOR TODAY

*Abba, Father, forgive us—the sinners that we are. Have mercy on us. We are not worthy of Your Son's sacrifice, and we never will be. Our hearts are heavy and full of sorrow as we recall His love and Your love. Please forgive us, and have mercy on our souls. In Jesus' name. Amen.*

# BECKY'S MEMORIES

## FOR YOU, MOM

My parents were never afraid to talk about death. In fact, as they grew older, death became a fairly popular topic of conversation. They felt that we children should be able to talk about it, too, so they took us to funerals and to the funeral homes to help us grasp the concept. To them death was a part of living and must not be shoved under the rug.

Our family talked about heaven a lot, too. Heaven was our goal and our focus. It was extremely important to our parents that our entire family make it to heaven. Mom frequently reminded us that she would get there first and wait for us. We had an expression: "We will meet at the gate." As her Alzheimer's progressed, she stopped remembering events, Scriptures, and names. However, she continued to remind me: "Remember, we will meet at the gate. The circle must not be broken."

Mom and Dad's love for each other was always strong. The idea of one of them being left behind was abhorrent to both of them. My mother often expressed a desire to die with my father. I would always groan, and say, "Mom, don't say that! How awful it would be for me if you two went at the same time. I couldn't handle that." Mom was not afraid of anything. She would reply, "Becky, death is instant. It would be wonderful if your daddy and I could step into eternity together. We cannot live without each other."

After Dad died, we had to put Mom in a nursing home with full care. You know, nursing homes are wonderful places; and nursing homes are horrible places. Entering those halls and searching for her in her wheelchair was agony for me. Mom had been such a vibrant woman with such a "presence." Like Edith Bunker from *All in the Family*, she ran everywhere she went. Now I had to look for her among those poor creatures with blank stares and short, white hair that all looked alike. Sometimes I did not even recognize her.

I sang to her when I visited, and sometimes she would sing with me. Mom loved music. She had a wonderful alto voice and enjoyed teaching the young girls at church to sing alto, too. She had been a music teacher and had an honest appreciation for all types of music. When she could no longer recognize any of her family members, she could still sing every word to:

Put another nickel in,
In the nickelodeon.
All I want is loving you
And music, music, music!

When we sang "I love you, a bushel and a peck," she always smiled.

Mom was safe in her world, but she looked like a lost little girl. Watching her tormented me. I prayed for her constantly. I lived at the Begging Place. I knew she wanted to go home. I fasted and begged God to take her home, and I asked others to beg, too. I know God heard our prayers. Seven months after Dad died, the nursing home called and said she was slipping away.

I started praying as I drove to the home. I entered her room, talking to her and kissing her. Her eyes were closed; she was completely unresponsive. However, about every five minutes, she opened her eyes, lifted her head, and peered into the distance. Then smiling, she laid her head down and closed her eyes. She was not fretting or anxious. She was very much at peace as she lay there, suspended between earth and Paradise. I stayed with her for several hours, just sitting there, trying to memorize her face and hands.

The sun set and darkness fell. The nurse came in and urged my husband and me to go and get something to eat. I remember saying, "But she needs someone to be with her." And the nurse said so kindly and gently, "She does have someone with her. We are here, and she could be like this for another day or even a week."

Jeff and I drove back home. Just as we started to eat supper, Mary, my mother's nurse called. She simply said to me, "Honey, your mama has gone to be with the angels." We drove back to the nursing home immediately and entered Mom's room. I kissed her and thanked God for His wonderful compassion and mercy. As we walked out of the nursing home, I was thankful that I did not have to enter its doors again. And I was so happy for Mom. Like Dad, she had won the victory. She had finally found her wings and flown away.

Mom was the most wonderful woman I have ever known, but more than that, she was the strongest Christian I have ever known. She loved the lost and would go anywhere, anytime to teach someone the gospel. As I stood beside her body in that nursing home, I knew she was then experiencing what she had lived for. Above all else, I knew this was not goodbye for either of us. We would see each other again.

Mom's journey was over. She was home at last, finally free from that horrible disease. She knew who she was, and she could see again. She was with our Savior, and she was with Dad once more. With His most tender mercies, God had granted her wish to die with Dad. They were only apart seven months. That's close enough.

Now I often wonder what Mom was looking at that day she died. She was not in any pain, but something was making her smile. I like to think there was a welcome committee in the distance. Perhaps Mom could see Dad and their close friends who had already passed over. Our Father tells us: "Precious in the sight of the Lord is the death of His godly ones" (Psalm 116:15).

We do not know what happens when one of God's children dies. We just have the comfort of this passage and the knowledge that the Lord considers our death as precious—cherished, treasured, and priceless. Death must be pretty wonderful. I don't know what Mom saw that day, but I do know it made her smile and brought her comfort.

Thank You, O God, for all of these things. Thank You for guiding all of us through this strange territory of life and death. Thank You for all the wonderful women that You have surrounded me with here on earth. And thank You for hearing all the prayers from the Begging Place in Mom's behalf. You are our Yahweh. You are our God and Father. And You are our rock.

Mom, I will miss you every day that I live on this earth without you. Thank you for your example, your dedication to God, your love for His Word, and your unconditional love for our family. I love you, and remember—I will meet you at the gate. That is a promise.

# EPILOGUE

*Be anxious for nothing, but in everything by prayer and
supplication with thanksgiving let your requests be
made known to God. And the peace of God, which
surpasses all comprehension, shall guard your
hearts and your minds in Christ Jesus
(Philippians 4:6-7).*

## GOD'S LITTLE GIRL

There is nothing more wonderful than being a Christian. In fact,
"wonderful" does not even begin to describe the privileges God gives
those who obey His gospel. To obey is joy, peace, security, and heaven. Not to obey is worry, insecurity, selfishness, and an eternal doom.
And we will choose whether or not to obey.

However, one aspect of being God's little girl is that our Father
has bestowed upon us continual encouragement: the blessing of
prayer. Prayer opens up the path between child and Parent in our
relationship with our Father. Prayer enables us to talk to the Father,
to praise Him, to seek Him, and to reveal what is on our heart. Prayer
is the avenue of communication that begins with us and ends with
God. And when there are times of deep distress in our lives, God even
grants us "begging rights."

> For all who are being led by the Spirit of God, these are sons of God.
> For you have not received a spirit of slavery leading to fear again,
> but you have received a spirit of adoption as sons by which we cry
> out, "Abba! Father!" (Romans 8:14–15).

In other words, God's little children don't have to live in fear but
are able to cry out "Abba, Father," just as Jesus did. Isn't it interesting
that the Holy Spirit inspired Paul to use the words "cry out"? Why
not just use the word "say"? Because Jesus cried out to His Father in
Gethsemane when He was praying at the Begging Place. He cried,
"Abba! Father! All things are possible for Thee; remove this cup from
Me; yet not what I will but what Thou wilt" (Mark 14:36). And when
we meet our Father at the Begging Place, we cry out, too.

## WHO BELONGS TO HIM?

Did God have to give us the avenue of prayer? Was God compelled to do so? Did He have to give us a way to communicate with Him? Of course not. God is all sufficient and does not need our prayers, neither does He need to talk to us. He chose to give us prayer so we could talk to Him. Prayer makes us feel better and enables us to lay our burdens at the Master's feet. Prayer gives us hope as we suffer with the many crises of life. We know our Father is listening, answering our prayers, and working out our problems because He loves His children.

Paul was inspired to write to Timothy: "Nevertheless, the firm foundation of God stands, having this seal, 'The Lord knows those who are His,' and 'Let everyone who names the name of the Lord abstain from wickedness'" (2 Timothy 2:19).

The message to Timothy and to all Christians is threefold:

1. God, our rock of Truth, will always stand firmly.

2. God has a seal; He knows who belongs to Him.

3. Live a righteous life and run from evil.

Study this passage and write it on your heart. It will bring comfort and peace in stressful times. God will not fail you; you can take that to the bank! "The Lord knows those who are His." He knows you belong to Him. He recognizes His little girls. That is comforting! Live as a Christian should—pure and right and holy.

And should you wonder how this corresponds with prayer, focus on this one thought: If God knows His children and everything about them, He knows what they are praying for. Trust in Him. Don't fret. He has it all handled and under control. Don't worry about tomorrow; God is already there!

## PRAY WITHOUT CEASING

Whatever you undertake, pray about it as God instructs: "Pray without ceasing" (1 Thessalonians 5:17). As we grow older in the faith, we learn what this Scripture is all about. It is what it is. It is as honest as it possibly can be: Pray continually.

I called my mother on the phone many times and asked her, "What are you doing?" She often said, "Why, honey, I am just sitting here praying and talking to the Lord."

When I was a young mother with two little ones strapped in their car seats, I often prayed aloud as I drove. Listen, it is scary out there on the highways, especially just outside Atlanta! I can still hear my voice saying things like: "O Father, please help me to be patient while I find a parking place!" "Dear Lord, please help us to be quiet and calm so I won't have a wreck." "O God, keep us safe." "Thank you, God!" I truly was learning to pray without ceasing.

Before long, two little voices in the backseat were saying about every ten minutes, "Thank you, God!" My friend, that is where it starts. If you want your children to know the Lord and to have a personal relationship with Him, start training them when they are babies. Teaching prayer to teenagers who are facing multiple catastrophes is difficult—sometimes impossible. Don't wait.

Gradually, as my children started school, there were more opportunities for them to experience the presence of God in their lives. Together we prayed for math tests, a teacher conflict, pop quizzes, and school friendships. We rejoiced together, too, as we saw their prayers answered. We always said, "Thank you, Lord!"

This experience helped us all to grow spiritually. And when, one day, I turned around and both my children had gone off to college, I knew that wherever they were, they were saying, "Thank you, Lord." Someone once said, " 'Pray without ceasing' means we can always run into our Father's heart."

## DEVOTED TO PRAYER

In his letter to the Christians at Rome, Paul urged them to serve God and each other. Take the time to read Romans 12; take it apart and write down all its commands and imperatives. Consider a small segment of that chaper:

> Be devoted to one another in brotherly love; give preference to one another in honor; not lagging behind in diligence, fervent in spirit, serving the Lord; rejoicing in hope, persevering in tribulation, devoted to prayer, contributing to the needs of the saints, practicing hospitality (Romans 12:10–13).

"Devoted to prayer." When we are devoted to something, we pursue it diligently. We are committed to it. We are dedicated to it. It is a part of our daily routine.

The New King James Version translates "devoted to prayer" as "continuing steadfastly in prayer." Christians who continue steadfastly in prayer are immoveable and surefooted in the doctrine of Jesus Christ. They know the strength that comes from communicating their desires and needs to the Father, and their deep, abiding faith continually seeks Him in prayer.

Burton Coffman says this about a passage from Romans 12:

> The glorious hope of the Christian is more than enough to flood the soul with rejoicing, even in the midst of abounding disappointments, provided it is kept in focus by the mind. This hope is the anchor of the soul (Hebrews 6:19) which enables the child of God to endure whatever storms may come, but not, however, without prayer. Prayer is the breathing of the redeemed soul, and the cessation or neglect of it will smother and destroy spiritual life (James Burton Coffman, *Commentary on Romans* [A.C.U. Press: Abilene, TX, 1973], 420).

Let's examine this concept "devoted to prayer" in a few more instances. Paul encouraged the Colossian Christians: "Devote yourselves to prayer, keeping alert in it with an attitude of thanksgiving" (Colossians 4:2). It was necessary to dedicate themselves to praying. It was necessary for Paul to stress the importance of praying to God continually to all the churches scattered around the globe. The early church's persecution was frightening and demanded constant supplication to God.

However, let's also notice the rest of this verse: "Keeping alert in it with an attitude of thanksgiving." Keeping alert in what? In the prayer that we are praying. How? With a thankful heart. In other words, while we are praying it is important to keep our minds sharp and aware of the things that we are saying which can prompt us to say thank you to our God. Have you ever remembered as you were praying that you needed to pray about something else or thank God for something you just remembered? I have. Paul is reminding us to be committed to praying, to be mentally alert while we pray, and to be thankful to God for all things. You know, it is possible to repeat the same prayer without thought. That is wrong. Our praying is not to be mechanical and methodical, but conscientious and heartfelt.

## DON'T FORGET TO SAY THANK YOU!

Do you recall your mother's prompting you to say thank you to an adult? How important are the words "thank you" to you? Don't you love to hear them from your children, no matter how old they are? Doesn't it bring you joy to receive a "thank you" note from a friend? Do you become resentful when your generosity is ignored, either by family members, co-workers, or friends? Of course you do. We all love to be appreciated for a kindness we have shown.

Kindnesses can be expensive. It costs money and time to shop for the right gift. Money is not easy to come by! Many times I have not had the funds to buy a gift for a bride or a new mother or a graduate. However, when I have purchased a special present, a "thank you" note has been important. Once I made a trip with two babies to the mall in the rain to buy a wedding present. The bride and groom never acknowledged it. Always remember to say thank you to those who are courteous. You do not know the circumstances that surrounded that lovely gift. Women want to hear the thank you.

## THE LORD WANTS TO HEAR THANK YOU TOO!

Frequently, we forget to say thank you to our Father. We put our requests before Him, and He answers our many prayers. How often do we remember to stop and thank Him for His marvelous kindness in the matter? God gave the world the most precious gift, His own Son. Have we acknowledged that gift? We ought to get down on our hands and knees every day and tell God how much we appreciate His incredible present.

Consider Jesus' healing of the ten lepers (Luke 17:12–19). Aren't you shocked by the ingratitude of the nine who never returned to say thank you? To have leprosy was to be isolated—until death. The Savior cleansed ten lepers so they could return to their families. Nine did not take the time to return and express their gratitude. The one who came back? Well, he was a Samaritan.

Do we act the same way by not acknowledging God's tender mercies as He daily listens to and answers our begging and pleadings? Too many times we neglect to tell God how much we love and appreciate Him for the blessings He pours on His children. Certainly we must seem like greedy and selfish kids!

Listen to what Paul said to the church at Philippi: "Be anxious for nothing, but in everything by prayer and supplication with thanksgiving let your requests be made known to God" (Philippians 4:6).

My mother used to quote this passage a lot. Then she found it in a newer translation: "Don't worry about anything, instead pray about everything. Tell God your needs, and don't forget to thank Him for His answers!" We forget to say, "Thank you, God," don't we?

## JESUS PRAYS FOR ME

Picture in your mind the last days of Christ on this earth. Ponder upon the upper room, the last supper, the Garden of Gethsemane, and the noisy, cowardly throng trying to arrest Jesus. On the night that the Lord's supper was instituted, Jesus had a warning for His friend and apostle Peter:

> "Simon, Simon, behold Satan has demanded permission to sift you like wheat; but I have prayed for you, that your faith may not fail; and you, when once you have turned again, strengthen your brothers." And he said to Him, "Lord, with You I am ready to go both to prison and to death!" And he said, "I say to you, Peter, the cock will not crow today until you have denied three times that you know Me" (Luke 22:31–34).

Peter was absolutely sure he would never deny his Master; Jesus was absolutely sure Peter would. Jesus knew Satan's power. Sifting wheat involves pounding stalks of wheat until only wheat remains. Satan wanted to pound the living daylights out of Peter. Can you feel the intense hatred that Satan had for Peter? But wait, there is more.

Jesus said, "But I have prayed for you." Prayed for you? Jesus had prayed for Peter to be strong and withstand whatever Satan intended to do to him. What a thrilling thought to consider! Jesus prayed for Peter, and Jesus can pray for us.

Satan wants to hurt those who love the Lord. Peter's situation is similar to another Bible incident. God asks Satan: "Have you considered My servant Job?" (Job 1:8). Satan replies that God has built a hedge around Job, but if his possessions were gone, Job would curse God. God gives Satan permission to hurt Job by taking his possessions, including his children, and smiting him with boils, but Job never curses God. If God gave Satan permission to hurt Job and if Satan demanded permission to inflict pain on Peter, does Satan ask permission from God to hurt us?

Jesus intercedes for us when we pray. He is our high priest. The Bible tells us so:

> Since then we have a great high priest who has passed through the heavens, Jesus the Son of God, let us hold fast our confession. For we do not have a high priest who cannot sympathize with our

weaknesses, but One who has been tempted in all things as we are, yet without sin (Hebrews 4:14–15).

But He, on the other hand, because He abides forever, holds His priesthood permanently. Hence, also, He is able to save forever those who draw near to God through Him, since He always lives to make intercession for them (Hebrews 7:24–25).

Christ's interceding for us is marvelous, but that is not the case here. There is no record here of Peter's asking Jesus to pray for him. Praying was Jesus' idea; He knew what Satan could do to a man.

Jesus is concerned about us; He knows how easy it is for us to fall. I am thrilled that Jesus is concerned about me and seeks the Father in prayer on my behalf, even when I have not asked Him to do so. What did we ever do to deserve His love and attention? Absolutely nothing.

## LET'S BEGIN ALL OVER AGAIN!

Do I pray every day? Am I a daily Bible reader? Do I study His Word? Do I seek the Lord and His will for me in my life? Do I pray for others as they experience sickness, trials, and death? Do I rejoice with those who rejoice and weep with those who weep? (Romans 12:15). Do I take this praying seriously? Do I know the Begging Place personally?

Brother Cato tells about brother Keeble's commitment to "praying without ceasing."

> Marshall Keeble knew the Lord, he knew life, and he loved both. Being a happy man in Christ, he enjoyed living and working for his Lord every day of life. Often Keeble would tell how good the Lord and life had been to him.
>
> Daily, Keeble would receive his power from God—and brother Keeble was a man of power. Whatever he did, he did mightily, for he knew he did it for the Lord . . .
>
> At age eighty-eight, brother Keeble said, "I get up in the middle of the night, just to thank God for letting me be alive. Most people my age are already dead, and here I am, still preaching the gospel. Thank God!" . . .
>
> In later years, brother Keeble would often arise during the night to seek the comforts of the bathroom. I would share the room with him and, each time he arose, I was awakened, though he never knew that I was. Never would he get back into bed until he had knelt by the bed and prayed (Cato, *His Hand and Heart*, 116–117).

Brother Keeble was a willing servant of God who realized who was in charge. God used him in a mighty way. What an impact his life and preaching have made on the church! Although he died in 1968, people are still talking about "Keeble."

Oh, my sisters, God has plans for you and me. He wants us to work for Him and to choose Him—not the world. In Him there is peace, rest, joy, happiness, and salvation—for us and for our children. When we go to the Begging Place over and over, we know Him, walk with Him, and live for Him.

Just to know that Jesus, my Savior, prays for me gives me hope beyond compare. Because of the Begging Place, we have a stronger and closer relationship with God. We return there again and again, knowing that prayer changes things. Our merciful Father meets us there, opens up His arms, and welcomes us home. We are in the presence of God—because He *is* the Begging Place!

## THOUGHTS TO PONDER

1. Why are Christians able to say "Abba! Father!" as Jesus did?

2. What does "pray without ceasing" mean to you?

3. What are some ways Christians can be ungrateful?

4. List new goals you have now for your prayer life.

## PRAYER FOR TODAY

*Dear Father, we approach Your throne now and give You all the glory for being who You are. You are our Father; our rock; our strength, our all sufficient God—El Shaddai, El Elohim, El Adonai, and most of all—our Yahweh. You are our God, and we are Your sheep. You have poured blessings down upon our head, and You have wrapped us in Your wonderful hedge and marvelous arms. For these things and so much more, we are eternally grateful. We are content to be where You are, and the world holds no glamour for us. Oh, love us forever and do not give up on us. We are Yours. And only Yours. Please let us walk by Your side. Lead us home, Father, lead us home. In Jesus' name. Amen.*

# PSALM 103

Bless the Lord, O my soul;
And all that is within me, bless His holy name.
Bless the Lord, O my soul,
And forget none of His benefits;
Who pardons all your iniquities;
Who heals all your diseases;
Who redeems your life from the pit;
Who crowns you with lovingkindness and compassion;
Who satisfies your years with good things,
So that your youth is renewed like the eagle.

The Lord performs righteous deeds,
And judgments for all who are oppressed.
He made known His ways to Moses,
His acts to the sons of Israel.
The Lord is compassionate and gracious,
Slow to anger and abounding in lovingkindness.
He will not always strive with us;
Nor will He keep His anger forever.
He has not dealt with us according to our sins,
Nor rewarded us according to our iniquities.
For high as the heavens are above the earth,
So great is His lovingkindness toward those who fear Him.
As far as the east is from the west,
So far has He removed our transgressions from us.
Just as a father has compassion on his children,
So the Lord has compassion on those who fear Him.
For He Himself knows our frame;
He is mindful that we are but dust.

As for man, his days are like grass;
As a flower of the field, so he flourishes.
When the wind has passed over it, it is no more;
And its place acknowledges it no longer.
But the lovingkindness of the Lord is from everlasting
To everlasting on those who fear Him,
And His righteousness to children's children,
To those who keep His covenant,
And who remember His precepts to do them.
The Lord has established His throne in the heavens;
And His sovereignty rules over all.
Bless the Lord, you His angels,
Mighty in strength, who perform His word,

Obeying the voice of His word!
Bless the Lord, all you His hosts,
You who serve Him, doing His will.
Bless the Lord, all you works of His,
In all places of His dominion;
Bless the Lord, O my soul!

## CLOSING SONG

## BLEST BE THE TIE THAT BINDS

Blest be the tie that binds
Our hearts in Christian love;
The fellowship of kindred minds
Is like to that above.

Before our Father's throne,
We pour our ardent prayers;
Our fears, our hopes, our aims are one,
Our comforts and our cares.

We share our mutual woes;
Our mutual burdens bear;
And often for each other flows
The sympathizing tear.

When we asunder part,
It gives us inward pain;
But we shall still be joined in heart,
And hope to meet again.

## THE BEGGING PLACE

Remember me, O God, remember I am but dust.
Remember me, O God, remember it is You that I trust.

Hold me closely, O Lord, close to Your heart.
Hold me tightly, O Lord, from You I will never depart.

I am just a little girl, O Father,
Who needs You every moment of the day.

I am Your little girl, O Father,
A daughter who has learned how to pray.

Come with me, my Father, we'll talk face to face,
We are here, my Father, we are at the Begging Place.

—Becky Blackmon

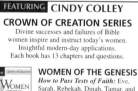